The Last Maori Wars

The Last Maori Wars

Two Accounts of the Conflicts in New Zealand During the 1860's

The Last Maori War in New Zealand
Sir George S. Whitmore

A Sketch of the New Zealand War
Morgan S. Grace

LEONAUR

The Last Maori Wars
Two Accounts of the Conflicts in New Zealand During the 1860's
The Last Maori War in New Zealand
by Sir George S. Whitmore
and
A Sketch of the New Zealand War
by Morgan S. Grace

FIRST EDITION

First published under the titles
The Last Maori War in New Zealand
and
A Sketch of the New Zealand War

Leonaur is an imprint of Oakpast Ltd

Copyright in this form © 2019 Oakpast Ltd

ISBN: 978-1-78282-872-3 (hardcover)
ISBN: 978-1-78282-873-0 (softcover)

http://www.leonaur.com

Contents

MAJOR-GEN. SIR G. S. WHITMORE, K.C.M.G., N.Z.M.

The Last Maori War in New Zealand

Contents

To the Memory of
The Late
Sir Frederick A. Weld, G.C.M.G.
And the Late
James Edward Fitzgerald, C.M.G.
The Recognised Authors
Of the Self-Reliant Policy
I Dedicate This Book

SIR F. A. WELD, G.C.M.G.   JAMES EDWARD FITZGERALD, C.M.G.

Preface

Self-reliance is the key with which the colonists of New Zealand have unlocked the two problems of war and settlement. Colonisation had begun under auspices unique in history. A powerful and warlike native race, struck by the superior advantages of civilization, voluntarily agreed to accept the sovereignty of the queen, reserving to itself the ownership of the soil, stipulating that all transfers should be to the Crown. The astonishing spectacle followed of a transfer of sovereignty without the aid of military force. The task undertaken by the first representative of the queen was apparently impossible.

The colonists were the minority; they were scattered along the coast at distant points, devoid of communication one with the other; they were ignorant of the customs and character of the native people; they knew nothing of the condition of their ownership of the soil, though the actual condition of their own existence as colonists was the acquisition of land. On the other hand, the Maori was strong and warlike, punctilious and generous, suspicious and shrewd, proud, and of singular independence. Yet the beginning of colonisation was prosperous, and the two races went side by side in friendship.

It was not in human nature, however, that this state of things could continue without friction. The leaders of colonisation were enlightened, and, above all things, alive to their duty of making good the promise of the British Ministry, which sanctioned the annexation of the country, that everything should be done to save the native people from the fate which in all history had befallen aboriginal races brought into contact with civilization. But many of the rank and file had no better conception of the proud and sensitive Maori than was implied in the degrading "n——r" theory, invariably applied by the unthinking Briton to all coloured races.

Many of the Maoris, too, were less clearsighted than their chiefs.

The friction between the races therefore grew harder as the possessions of the white race increased. Its first result was Heke's war, which exploded the Maori theory of the invincibility of the *Pakeha* soldier. In this war some of the great chiefs were on our side, and their people fought loyally for the supremacy to which they had voluntarily submitted.

The European shortly after obtained self-government, but the exigencies of constitutional rule of the British pattern led inevitably to neglect of Maori interests. The land purchases of the Europeans proceeded, in spite of the good intentions of their best men, faster than the schemes for the amelioration of the Maori people. A section of the great chiefs in course of time adopted the views which had driven Heke into the field. The result was the King movement, at the head of which was placed Te Whero Whero, the greatest friend the *Pakeha* had up to that time possessed. The two races drifted, by natural process of increasing misunderstanding, into war. The northern part of New Zealand saw an army of 14,000 British troops in the field, engaged in the work of wrestling with Maori insurrection. The Maoris were not united, however, for many took our side. The Colonial Government at the same time levied troops in the Waikato, and raised money. In the aggregate, 17,000 men were available, besides native auxiliaries, for the work of restoring the queen's supremacy.

The period from 1861 to 1864 had seen New Zealand filled with royal troops, and many little actions had been fought against the Maoris with more or less success, but there seemed to be but faint prospect of conquering, or of peace. On the contrary, the area of war seemed to be widening, and unhappily a difference of opinion arose between the two Imperial officers in the colony, which, to a great extent, paralysed all progress. The Colonial Parliament had with no niggard hand strained its means to the utmost to assist and facilitate the Royal operations, and it seemed to the colonists that, if they had to pay and support the three Waikato regiments, as well as the whole cavalry and the steamers, it would be as well to bear the entire cost of the war, which in that case they would direct and control. It was on this account that a most loyal colony resolved to invite the Imperial Government to withdraw its troops, and leave New Zealand to work out its own salvation.

The impatience of the colonial public found an expression in various speeches of the celebrated James Edward Fitzgerald. The policy therein outlined was adopted by Mr. (afterward Sir Frederick) Weld, when he became Prime Minister. On being summoned by Sir George Grey to form a Ministry, he placed upon paper his views in that direction, amounting in short to a request to the Home Government to withdraw its troops, and to leave the subjugation of the native in colonial hands.

In 1865 the petition of the colony was submitted to Parliament, and the discussion which followed is well worthy of perusal in the altered state of public opinion, and entitles New Zealand to claim to have initiated the true Imperial spirit when she adopted her policy of self-reliance.

The usual debate in the House of Commons resulted in the acceptance of this wholly novel undertaking on the part of this small and distant colony to relieve the Mother Country of a burden which an expensive campaign had proved her to be wholly incapable of bearing to success. The astonishing point in the story for readers of today is the manner in which this debate was arranged—in which, in fact, a hearing was secured for the colonial petition at all. Mr. Cardwell told one of our colonists that "he hoped that the colony would feel flattered that so large a House was assembled on this occasion, unique in the records of Parliament, when an Indian or colonial question was before it. It was by a promise that the debate would be over by dinner time."

The colony was actually asked, in perfect good faith, to "feel flattered" at having, in a matter vitally touching its welfare, obtained the favour of a perfunctory debate.

Such were our relations with the Mother Country then. Now the whirligig of time offers us a contrast in the treatment accorded, in 1900, by both Houses, and by all degrees of statesmen to the Australian Commonwealth Bill—a measure not more important to Australia at the later date than the policy so bravely sketched in the petition of 1865 was to New Zealand then. That contrast gives us the exact measure of the improvement that has taken place in the interval, in the relations between Downing Street and the great colonial dependencies of the Crown. It is the difference between "cutting the painter" and the maintenance of the Empire intact and glorious.

Whatever may have been the opinion in the colony is immaterial. But the main feature of the debate was the question whether the little colony would or would not pay £40 a man for the services of the Royal troops for the past two years. This may be fairly considered as the spirit with which England then regarded her infant colonies. New Zealand had incurred in these two years a debt of three millions of money, to defray the expenses of 3000 infantry, 300 cavalry, and a swarm of steamers, to say nothing of the native contingents, to facilitate the operations of the Imperial general and his 14,000 troops. The petition of the colony was certainly not adopted graciously by Parliament, which had forgotten that the colony undertaking this great task had only 150,000 people. The sum of three millions had been borrowed by the colony in order to pay for the three Waikato regiments and other military expenditure incurred in order to assist the military, and on the governor's suggestion a promise had been given to the men so enlisted of grants of land according to rank in the force.

To obtain the land legally, from which such grants could be made, it was essential that an Act should be passed confiscating the necessary area. To this Sir George Grey would not assent, and one Ministry had resigned in consequence. After a considerable interregnum, as there was a disinclination on the part of many leading men to accept office, at last Mr. F. Weld agreed to try. He, however, insisted on a written promise from Sir George Grey that he would concede the confiscation of the land, thus enabling him to keep faith with the military settlers and so to discharge them when no longer required; following this up with the respectful petition to the Imperial Government to be allowed henceforward to keep the peace for itself.

This was a singular step for so small and poor a colony, but as things then stood, there was hardly any alternative. Mr. Weld at once undertook the task of self-reliance, and on the East Coast and Bay of Plenty put down the local disturbances with purely colonial troops. The operations undertaken by Mr. Weld had been forced upon him by natives from distant parts of the colony, and were completely successful, and a large number of prisoners were left in the hands of the government, whom they decided to ship off to the Chatham Islands.

The rebellion began to dwindle away through 1864, but broke out again in 1866, when a sudden inroad of armed natives descended upon the western frontier of the till then peaceful province of Hawke's Bay, in the early part of the month of October, and seized a friendly native village and some cattle of the settlers. Mr. Weld was no longer in power, and had been succeeded by Mr. Stafford, who, however, had left the agency in the hands of Mr. McLean, a follower of his, and a Hawke's Bay settler, who, moreover, was entrusted with the Governor's power to call out the militia for actual service. There were no troops in the province at all, with the exception of about twenty men who had strict orders not to leave the centres of population, and to act only on the defensive.

In a distant part of the province there was a force of some twenty or thirty men of the lately raised armed constabulary, who were sent for, and arrived just in time, but this force did not make it unnecessary to call out the militia, who were the tradesmen and artificers of the small town and its suburbs. It was very much against the grain that McLean took the strong step of calling out the militia. But there was so clearly a necessity for firmness, and his advisers were so unanimous, that at last he consented, and directed Lieut.-Colonel Whitmore to draw out the local forces and restore order. The action which followed was very complete. Some thirty or more were killed and buried on the ground, as many more were wounded and removed in carts, while the rest were marched into town and confined in the gaol.

For nearly two years the Hawke's Bay lesson sufficed to keep the peace, and the colony began to think her troubles over for good, but the calm of 1866 proved to be only the precursor of storm. The confiscation of the necessary land to locate the military settlers had been by this time carried out in the Waikato district, and had been proclaimed on the West Coast; and, as far as the Waikato was concerned, seemed to be accepted by the local Maoris. On the West Coast, however, things did not run so smoothly, where the armed constabulary and some local levies hurriedly raised were completely defeated under Colonel McDonnell, with heavy loss. However, the colony pulled itself together, and faced the position, the troops in the field were to a great extent reorganised, another officer was placed in command, and the colonists were anxious to prove that they were in earnest about colonial self-reliance.

Up to this time the colony had discharged all the duties which had hitherto been recognised as the especial obligation of the parent State, and the position of things now looked so much more grave, that not a few persons conceived that the task was beyond the ability of the colony. The colony of the Cape, in its many native wars, had always looked to England for support, both in men and money. It was in 1868, a year that will not be forgotten, that wool, the great staple of the colony, had fallen so much in price that it hardly paid to shear the sheep, and money was at famine price, that this terrible addition to ordinary expenditure fell upon New Zealand. When neither public nor private means were at all easy, an undefined and certainly enormous expenditure had to be faced. In the Ballarat riots England had provided the troops and the money.

New Zealand had, however, deliberately absolved the Mother Country from her responsibility. Of all Colonies, this was the youngest, and nearly the poorest; but it was an Anglo-Saxon community, and accepted the self-imposed task willingly, if not cheerfully. Of course, there were individuals in the community who shook their heads, and looked forward doubtfully at the ability of the colony to carry out its undertakings. But these were only a few. The great majority recognised the obligation, notwithstanding the commercial crisis the colony was at the moment passing through. Land, at the moment, in all the pastoral colonies, was more a liability than an asset, and it did not require any great financial perspicacity to recognise that New Zealand had undertaken her liability at a most unfortunate time. Such was the position in which the colony found itself when it was suddenly confronted with the task of restoring peace.

The story of the wars that followed is told in the following pages.

There is no need to refer to the story in detail. In so distinguished a case it will be enough to quote the official commendation. In the governor's speech opening the Parliament of 1869, on June 1st, there is the following passage:—

> The thanks of the colony are due to Colonel Whitmore and to the officers and men of the colonial forces, European and native, for the conspicuous courage with which they have encountered the enemy whenever he presented himself, and for the indomitable energy and zeal with which they have tracked and dispersed his retreating forces; arduous and harassing duties, in the course of which they have penetrated forests and inhospitable wilds hitherto unvisited by any European force, and inaccessible to the ordinary means of transport. The difficulties they have surmounted have had no parallel in the military history of this country. No troops could have displayed a more gallant spirit; no officers could have conducted campaigns with more enterprise, skill, and prudence.

That eloquent tribute was immediately endorsed by Parliament. The next month brought out a despatch from the Secretary of State to the Governor of the colony. The governor, moved by his responsible advisers, had recommended Colonel Whitmore for well-earned decoration. The despatch must be quoted *in extenso:*—

No. 84.—Despatch from the Earl Granville, K.G., to Governor Sir G. F. Bowen, G.C.M.G.

Downing Street, July 13th, 1869.

Sir—I have received your despatch, No. 44, of April 3rd last, conveying a recommendation in favour of Colonel George Stoddart Whitmore, of the New Zealand Colonial Forces, for the distinction of a Companion of the Order of St. Michael and St. George, in consideration of his military services to the colony.

I have before remarked with satisfaction on the skill and energy with which Colonel Whitmore has conducted the military operations which have been entrusted to him, and I have had much pleasure in submitting his name to the queen for this mark of the Royal approval, which Her Majesty has graciously directed me to offer him.

I have, &c.,

(Signed) Granville.

The passage of the governor's letter to which the above was a reply is worth quoting. Sir G. F. Bowen wrote:

I venture to express an earnest hope that the Companionship of the Order of St. Michael and St. George will be conferred on Colonel Whitmore, for this mark of Her Majesty's approval, while fairly earned by him personally, cannot fail to be an encouragement to the colonial forces, on which has now been cast the entire weight of the active suppression of the formidable rebellion against the authority of the queen that has been so long raging in this country. Moreover, it will be remembered that the Companionship of the Bath has been conferred during the Maori wars on several officers of Her Majesty's naval and military forces, who, meritorious as their conduct was, have not had the opportunity of commanding on such important and difficult services, as the capture of Ngatapa, and other services performed by Colonel Whitmore.

At the present time Colonel Whitmore has under his command in the Wanganui and Taranaki districts (according to the 'States' of March 31st *ult.*), 1348 officers and men of the colonial forces (chiefly of the armed constabulary), together with 405 friendly natives, making in all a total of less than 2000 men. Now, it will be remembered that in 1865, only four years ago, General Cameron had under his command in the same district and against the same hostile clans, no less than 4497 officers and men of

Her Majesty's regular troops, in addition to detachments of the colonial forces, making up a total of above 6000 men.... It will further be remembered that Generals Cameron and Chute had at their disposal the material aid of the Commissariat and of the Military Train, and of a strong detachment of the Royal Artillery; whereas Colonel Whitmore has no Commissariat Service or Land Transport Corps, and only a few small Cohorn mortars, that are carried on pack-horses, or (as happened at the capture of Ngatapa) in the arms of his men, over mountains and through forests inaccessible to horses.

In proof of the vitality of the Self-Reliant movement, it may be mentioned that the colony did not stop short in its preparations for defence. In 1885, during the so-called "Russian scare," the government called upon the same officer to organise its defences against possible aggression from abroad, and to arm its principal sea-ports against attack. This was done under Colonel Whitmore's personal superintendence, at a total cost to the Colony of half a million sterling; and, concurrently therewith, 12,000 volunteers were embodied for the defence of New Zealand. Through this organisation, when the danger of foreign invasion had passed, the military spirit survived in the colony and formed the nucleus upon which the Contingents for South Africa were afterwards based.

In all this story there is only one thing less astonishing than the brilliancy of Colonel Whitmore's services. It is the calm satisfaction with which the governor and Secretary of State limited themselves to the reward granted him. But we need not pursue the subject. The times, fortunately, are altered. Colonel Whitmore got the thanks of the Parliament that knew his work, and his services are an imperishable record.

In the vivid narrative of Sir George Whitmore there are many things remarkable. But of all these, none is more remarkable than the key-note of "self-reliance." The campaigns described were fought by colonial troops; they were paid for by colonial means; and they were attended by a success that made racial war in New Zealand for ever impossible. The two races are now one people, equal in loyalty to the Royal house.

Nothing can be more striking than the proof afforded of this fact by the great welcome given by the Maori people to their Royal Highnesses the Duke and Duchess of York at Rotorua in June, 1901, during the Royal tour through New Zealand. It was a welcome remarkable not only for its warmth and generosity, but for the thorough loyalty of chiefs and people. Among the prominent chiefs who attended on that occasion, as amongst the great *tauas* (war parties) which performed their war dances with such fervour, there were many who had fought with us and against us. The daughter of the chivalrous Kemp (Rangi-hiwinui), who had done so much, was at the head of her tribe; Pokiha Taranui, who, like Kemp, had attained the rank of major in our service, and been rewarded by the queen with a sword of honour, was with her.

So were the Ngatiporo, the tribe of the valiant Ropata, also a major and the recipient of a sword of honour, who, before he died, sat in the Legislative Council; and the tribe was under the leadership of Ropata's right-hand man in all his wars, Tuta Niho Niho, who flourished the sword of honour which he, too, had won from the queen's hand. With them, and no whit inferior in loyalty and enthusiasm, or in generosity and courtesy whole-souled, were such men as Hori Ngatai, who had commanded against us at the Gate pah; Tamaikowha, chief of the Uriwera, who had been the life and soul of the historic Orakau defence; Patara, who had fought in the Maori van at Rangiriri; Turoa, who had escaped from the slaughter of Moutoa, and many a *Hau-Hau* who had been out with Titokowaru and Te Kooti in the latter days. Men who had spent years in stalking one another in the bush, met in contented amity under the shadow of the great *Pax Britannica*. It was a noble evidence of the success of our self-reliant policy.

One word as to the treatment experienced at our hands by the Maori race, so valiant in war, both against us and for us. That so many fought on our side is some proof, surely, of the high-minded fidelity of the colonists to the promise of amelioration authoritatively given to the race when it agreed to accept our supremacy. But about the others, a few words are necessary.

Among the objections made by members of the House of Commons to the petition of the colony in 1866, was the argument of those who were called the Philo-Maori party, who—then, as in these days do the Pro-Boer party, who will believe anything against their countrymen—affected to think that the colony only wished to oppress the natives and rob them of their land. Since then, with every power in their hands, the country has prospered. The natives have been justly and even generously treated, and their numbers have steadily increased, till the census of this year shows an increase of ten *per cent*, in their population.

While this has been going on, four Maoris have, under the law of representation, had seats in the representative branch, and two in the nominated branch of the Legislature. Surely with the example of the Transvaal before their eyes, some who took part in that debate, will regret their action of thirty-five years ago, and hesitate to suspect their own kin of intentions so unworthy of our race. Another point in the discussion should be mentioned, because it was especially ungenerous and unwise. During the past two years, the British Government had maintained a force of 14,000 men in the colony, and it was mainly because the results had proved so small and the colony had been required to do so much in addition, that it had sent its petition to Parliament at all. But one feature of the debate turned upon the question of whether the colony could not be made to pay £40 a man for the services of these men in the past!

In addition, returning to the Maori, there are many schools for the Maori people, special laws have been passed giving them the management of their land, and the local government of their communities. Maoris have taken degrees in the university, diplomas in medicine, places at the Bar, and orders in various Churches. There is a young Maori party, well educated, and earnestly working for the amelioration of their people. Aperana Ngata, a barrister of the Supreme Court, and M.A. of the university, a litterateur of considerable powers; Dr. Pomare, a distinguished bacteriologist; Hone Heke, the capable representative, are all examples of what education has done for the Maori. The wealth and culture of many Maori proprietors is a commonplace of various districts of the North Island.

Last, but not least, the Minister at the head of native affairs, the Hon. James Carroll, is of the Maori race, and one of the most capable men in the colony. These things explain the loyalty and enthusiasm exhibited at Rotorua by all the Maori chiefs and tribesmen who were once arrayed against us in the field. These are the fruits of self-reliance, of which that ungraciously received petition of 1866 was the beginning.

There is another fruit. When the Empire needed men for the war in South Africa, New Zealand was the first colony to spring to arms. It was not a question of asking. The flower of the Colonial youth came forward with eagerness on every centre of population, from the North Cape to the Bluff. From first to last we sent 8000 horsemen, a larger proportion beyond comparison than any other colony of the Empire, into the field, where they showed themselves soldiers of bravery and capacity, possessing the instinct of discipline, the high sense of duty, the keenness of enterprise, the *esprit de corps,* the patriotism, in short all the qualities which come to soldiers from high traditions. These are the traditions made by their fathers in campaigns on their own soil. In 1866 our statesmen appealed to the public spirit of the best colonists who ever left the shores of the United Kingdom. They responded by putting down the troubles of their own household in a manner which qualified them for bringing substantial ungrudging help to the Empire in the hour of need.

We sent, from first to last, 8000 men to South Africa, and during the Royal tour we showed our Royal visitors many thousands more of the same sturdy stamp. Every street in the four centres was lined with our soldiery to receive their Royal Highnesses: in every procession large bodies of mounted troops accompanied the Royal carriage: at Christchurch alone 12,000 soldiers and cadets marched past the Duke of York and the Royal standard, many of them from districts renowned in Maori war: and there was not a single paid soldier in all these gatherings. The self-reliance of 1866 has made New Zealand formidable to the invader and valuable to the Empire.

R. A. L.

Introduction

The first rumours of the unexpected and sanguinary repulse suffered by colonial troops at Ngutuotemanu, on the West Coast, fell upon the public and upon the Parliament then in session with a perfectly unwarrantable consternation. The feeling of alarm was fomented by daily reports published in the press from the narratives of survivors (many of whom were deserters) and their sensational correspondents. The truth was that underlying the professions of confidence in the "self-reliant policy," which some believed in, and the colony had adopted with a flourish of trumpets, there really existed among many, perhaps a majority of the people, considerable distrust of our ability to carry out operations in the field, without imperial military assistance and direction.

Those who felt this doubt, regarded the alarming intelligence hourly arriving as a confirmation of their secret opinions and distrust, and of these many asserted that Mr. Weld's policy, in which they had hitherto acquiesced, had broken down, and urged the necessity of reversing it and appealing to the Home Government for assistance.

The most senseless panic appeared to seize all classes, and seemed to grow in intensity in proportion to the distance from the only seat of danger. At the front, in Taranaki, the settlers braced themselves once more to face the worst, but along the coast the alarm grew mile by mile, till in Wellington itself there were some who expected from day to day to see the advance of Titokowaru's band, then only seventy in number, taking possession of the suburbs of the city. It was during this excitement, and when Parliament itself had shown as yet no spirit worthy of the crisis, that Mr. McLean brought forward his alarm resolutions. These were so called from the few first words they contained:—"That this House has learned with alarm, &c." The opposition in 1868 had been obstructive and factious to a degree.

The condition of the country, never so critical as then, weighed as nothing to such patriots as Mr. Fox, who thought he saw in the difficulties of the government, an opportunity to overturn and supplant it. He had already proposed two votes of confidence, which resulted only in exposing his own want of public spirit and impatience by any means to gain office. Both were defeated by substantial majorities, and even Mr. Fox would probably have hesitated to bring down a third, had not Mr. McLean opportunely afforded him the opening. Mr. McLean's resolutions could only be treated by the government as a third challenge, and Mr. Stafford accordingly at once picked up the glove that was thrown down.

Mr. McLean was a self-raised man, who had for years lived among the Maoris, and acquired their language. He understood them well, and knew all their superstitions, traditions, songs, and modes of thought. Having been subsequently long employed by government, and entrusted with large sums of money for the purchase of native land, he acquired a considerable influence over the native race, who saw in him the distributor of nearly all the money they could at that time acquire. He was, too, highly qualified to deal with Maoris. His bulky presence, to which they attached much importance, impressed them. His address and manner were pleasing to them, and he represented in their eyes the government of the colony.

For many years he had been Native Secretary as well as purchaser of native lands. Under the regime of those days when the control of native affairs was retained by the Crown, the funds which enabled him to carry out his duties were supplied by Parliament it is true, but Mr. McLean enjoyed under a dual government a *quasi*-independence. When a native war sprang up in 1860, through a disputed land purchase, it necessarily entailed great sacrifices on the settlers, although they had no voice in the conduct of the military operations. It was almost impossible under such circumstances that Mr. McLean should escape very unfair and often ungenerous attack. In Parliament the opposition thundered against him, the press and public condemned him, and at last Mr. Stafford, who had consistently supported him, had to make a cabinet question of his defence from the bitter attacks upon his character and conduct in Parliament.

By a small majority the opposition was defeated, but the public feeling against Mr. McLean grew in intensity, till, when Mr. Stafford was himself outvoted in 1861, Mr. Fox at once broke up Mr. McLean's department and relegated him to private life. Retiring to Hawke's Bay, where he had acquired considerable pastoral property, Mr. McLean became successively superintendent of that province, member for the town and district of Napier, and under Mr. Stafford (when he became once more Premier), agent for the General Government on the East Coast. This last flattering appointment made Mr. McLean practically an irresponsible dictator within his pro-consulate of Hawke's Bay, and what is now Cook Country. He had almost all the power of the whole Cabinet, with none of its responsibility, and, uniting as he did in his own person the offices of chief magistrate of the province and member for the district, he wielded a larger influence than any other single person in the colony.

Soon after his election to the House of Representatives, Mr. McLean took his seat among Mr. Stafford's supporters, and there was probably no man in the House upon whose loyal support Mr. Stafford had a better right to rely; yet when the time came to have in some measure repaid his obligation, and in his turn to give yeoman's service to his chief, it was reserved for Mr. McLean to play the part of Brutus to his Caesar, Mr. Stafford. Metternich once said, after the war in Hungary had been ended through the aid of Russia, that Austria would one day astound the world by the immensity of her ingratitude, and truly when she joined the Western Alliance against Russia in 1854, she justified that prediction. To compare small things with great, not less did Mr. McLean in 1868 surprise Parliament and shock his friends by his unexpected and ungrateful tergiversation and by his alliance with his heretofore implacable enemy, Mr. Fox.

The "alarm resolutions" came at an unfortunate moment for Mr. Stafford, and almost succeeded through fortuitous circumstances. Mr. McLean in changing sides took with him his friend and colleague, Mr. Ormond, and his pocket Maori vote the chief Tareha. These defections though counting six in a division, important in a small House, would not of themselves have sufficed to make a really close division, but as it happened, the Taranaki members, in whose district the hostilities were actually occurring, objected strongly to the authority and control of military affairs at the front being vested in Lieut.-Colonel McDonnell, to whose incapacity they attributed the late disaster to our arms, which so greatly endangered their province.

Their mouthpiece was Major Atkinson, and at an interview with Mr. Stafford he stated that he regarded Lieut.-Colonel McDonnell as quite incapable of commanding European troops, with whom he had never been much connected, or of conducting independent opera-

27

tions in the field at all.

That being their view, they demanded that officer's immediate removal or dismissal, as a condition of their continuing to vote with what had been their party; but Mr. Stafford was, like the late Lord Palmerston, a statesman who never would abandon a subordinate until convinced of his unfitness or his fault. Lieut.-Colonel McDonnell's report had not yet been received. All that was known of the misfortune he had met with was on the authority of deserters, or nameless writers unworthy of belief. Consequently, and without a moment's hesitation, Mr. Stafford positively declined to make any such pledge, even at the cost of losing more members from his side. Still, it was a matter of doubt how the majority might go, and therefore Mr. Fox, who knew exactly the value of every vote just then, resorted to a very unworthy expedient to secure a victory for the resolutions.

Of the many eloquent and highly educated men who formerly adorned the House of Representatives of New Zealand, none was ever so perfect a master of vituperative invective as Mr. (afterwards Sir William) Fox. In early times he had used this weapon against Mr. McLean with a violence and virulence that created a sympathy with that gentleman. Now he brought it to bear upon the Defence Minister, the high-souled Colonel Haultain, whom he lashed for not having yet proceeded to the front.

When, however, Lieut.-Colonel McDonnell's reports had been received, and Colonel Haultain asked for the usual courtesy of a pair in order to go there, Mr. Fox tried to gain a vote by refusing it. Happily, however, Mr. Fox was not successful, for his old friend, the Bayard of the House, Dr. Featherston, saved him from the disgrace of winning a division in such a manner, and gave his own personal pair to the Defence Minister. Yet, and notwithstanding all the favouring circumstances, Mr. McLean's resolutions were not carried, though the government escaped defeat only by the Speaker's casting vote.

At a largely attended meeting of his followers. Mr. Stafford was with difficulty persuaded to carry on the government, and the Ministry did not resign, though to carry on the government in face of so violent an opposition was a task that few would have coveted.

I felt so strongly that the public had made up its mind too quickly as regarded Lieut.-Colonel McDonnell, that I addressed at this time an appeal to all reasonable people who had kept their heads in the calamity which had already cost us so many valuable lives, to withhold their judgment a little while, till the facts were known, and as

Lieut.-Colonel McDonnell had lost so many officers, I volunteered, though his senior, to proceed to Patea with Colonel Haultain, and serve under his orders till he was provided with sufficient assistance. I left, therefore, with Colonel Haultain, and for a short time remained with Colonel McDonnell at the front.

Colonel Haultain remained long enough at Patea to satisfy himself that the consequences of the late defeat at Ngutu-o-te-manu rendered it absolutely impossible to avoid a retrograde movement. He discussed the question alone with Lieut.-Colonel McDonnell (I having been sent to Turu-turu-mokai), and in the end a retreat from our advanced post at Waihi to Patea, a distance of over twenty miles, with outposts at Manawapo and Kakaramea, was decided upon. Unfortunately, at this juncture Lieut.-Colonel McDonnell was compelled to leave for Wanganui, where very melancholy family circumstances required his presence.

Hardly, however, had he left Patea, before Colonel Haultain was compelled to disband No. 5 (Major von Tempsky's) Division of armed constabulary, which positively refused to serve any longer unless Lieut.-Colonel McDonnell was removed. Of course, dictation on such a subject could not be listened to. As Honorary Officer Commanding on the East Coast, I had advised the government to withdraw from Napier, and send to the West Coast the division (No. 1 A.C.) I had myself raised there, replacing it with a new Division to be recruited for the purpose. Patea was in presence of the enemy, Napier was not, and as there was no other force in the colony available, it seemed to me that it would be wiser to train a new division in an undisturbed than in a disturbed district, face to face with danger.

It was fortunate that my advice was acted upon and the intact and reliable division under Major Fraser brought speedily round to Patea, for the volunteers hurriedly engaged for three months were quite untrained and wholly demoralised by casualties, defeat, and loss of officers. The remaining shreds of No. 2 and No. 3 Divisions A.C. were few in number, No. 5 was disbanded, No. 4 compelled to defend Waikato, and the skeleton remnant of two divisions was utterly inadequate alone to prevent the advance of the victorious band of Titokowaru, which each day augmented. Notwithstanding, however, the manifest and unavoidable necessity of the reinforcement of Patea by No. 1 A.C., the action of the government was most unreasonably resented by the public of Hawke's Bay, and an agitation arose, excited by Mr. McLean, whose hostility to the government since his defeat knew no bounds.

Mr. Stafford had attributed Mr. McLean's defection to the fact that he had demanded that a large sum (£56,000) should be placed practically at his own uncontrolled disposal in order to provide against any possible outbreak on the East Coast. As, however, he would not or could not state, except in vague general terms, for what purpose the money was required, Mr. Stafford declined unless he chose to accept the responsibility of defending the expenditure as a Cabinet Minister. This, however, did not suit Mr. McLean, and he took the refusal of his extraordinary demand in extremely ill part. The removal of the fifty constables without his consent being asked, he chose to consider an outrage, though why he thought so was inexplainable; and the ill-feeling fomented by him and his friends at this period was manifested in a series of public and private attacks upon the government of the day till its defeat a year later, and upon myself and others after Mr. Stafford had retired, which for persistence and vindictiveness have rarely been equalled in colonial history.

It was under such difficulties, and without a military force, that Mr. Stafford had to undertake the most arduous campaign the colony had yet experienced on both coasts of the island almost simultaneously. With a scantily furnished treasury, with intrigue rampant even in the lines of the soldiery, and passive resistance amongst the most trusted *employés* of the government, we took the field under every discouraging circumstance that could have existed in the extremity of the colony; in fact, there was so little national spirit that the sword was almost rendered powerless by the shameful conduct of a few political adventurers who hungered for office, and hoped if they could cause Mr. Stafford's failure to profit by his discredit or disgrace.

CHAPTER 1

Urewera Mountains and Outbreak at Poverty Bay

If upon a map of the North Island of New Zealand a parallelo-gram is described of which the shores of the coast from Napier to the East Cape, and from the East Cape to Whakatane are the Eastern and Northern sides, while the road from Napier to Opepe and a line thence to Whakatane, by the valley of the Rangitaiki, are the South-ern and Western ones, a district will be enclosed, dominated by the beetling heights of the Uriwera Mountains, which fill up the great bulk of the area. Those forest-clad ranges, high, cold, and precipitous, have since all record, afforded a safe refuge to the wild and primitive tribe to which they belong. Within them there is neither open space nor plain, and but few clearings for cultivation.

The owners of the soil are not an industrious race, and they have never raised more crop than was absolutely indispensable for their support. Such spots as they have annually cleared and cultivated are situated in the narrow valleys, torn out by the mountain torrents, of which many considerable ones flow into the plain country outside. They have all shale and boulder bottoms, and form the only practi-cable approaches to the principal settlements.

Snow and rain fall so frequently in that high country that these streams are constantly flooded, remaining sometimes impassable for weeks at a time, and during such periods the Uriwera warrior can rest in security and laugh at invasion from without. In 1868 this district was almost a *terra incognita* to the Europeans, few of whom had ever penetrated the mountains, notwithstanding the Britannic love of travel and discovery. Of those few Mr. Hunter Brown, of Nelson, late R.M. of Wairoa, was the only one who had ever left any record of his experi-

ences, but his description was accurate and valuable as far as it went.

From their eyrie heights the Uriweras looked down disdainfully upon the fat plains of Ahuriri, Turanga, Waiapu, Opotiki, and Whakatane, strips of rich land intervening between their fastness and the sea. They felt no envy of the greater productiveness of the soil, for they had no desire to labour to obtain the reward of industry which they despised. They were mountaineers who had bidden defiance to Hongi the Conqueror, who scorned men who felt fatigue in mounting acclivities at an angle of 45 degrees *or none*, and who always could procure such food as they required by the chase.

In the pursuit of the wild pigs and birds of the forest they were *facile princeps* among Maoris, and their forests team with this kind of life. In 1868 they were, of all New Zealand tribes, the most adventurous and the hardiest. In the fight they had the reputation of reckless bravery; in war they were swift of foot and were the only night-marching tribe, from which they acquired the soubriquet of "*Uriwera haere po.*" They had in 1862 sent a contingent to the Waikato to help Rewi, and it was from the throat of an Uriwera warrior at Orakau that the proud and defiant reply was hurled back to the British summons to surrender, "We will continue to fight ever, ever, ever."

That they kept their word at the cost of their lives, that but an insignificant remnant ever returned to tell the tale of the heroism of the war party, was nothing to the tribe. They had distinguished themselves even among the proud Waikatos, they had proved in the open field that they were bravest where all were brave; and this sufficed to their friends, and the *tangi* for the slain became a war song of triumph rather than a wail of sorrow.

Such were the Uriweras and such their inhospitable country when in 1869, after great provocation and for the safety of the coast settlements, the government of New Zealand undertook the task of reducing these sturdy mountaineers to subjection by force of arms. When on July 10th, 1868, Te Kooti returned to New Zealand in the *Rifleman* from the Chatham Islands with 163 other escaped prisoners, and their women and children 135 in number, he landed at Whareongonga, some few miles south of Young Nick's Head, the southern point of Turanga or Poverty Bay.

The prisoners brought with them all the arms they were able to get at the Chathams, but the supply was scanty enough; they had with them only thirty-two public and private rifles and fowling-pieces with seven revolvers, and when they landed they brought on shore besides a

quantity of ammunition and accoutrements (see appendix H.R.A.15 1868) and large stores of flour, sugar and tobacco, &c.

The settlers of Turanga, and indeed of the whole colony, were taken by surprise, for the escape of the prisoners had been wholly unforeseen. At first, negotiation was resorted to by the R.M., Major Biggs, but without success, the prisoners refusing to surrender themselves or their arms. Te Kooti had by this time acquired immense influence over his followers, and had declared himself the prophet of a new religion. Partly through their predisposition to superstitious fanaticism, and partly through their fears—for his rule was severe, and he had already executed one of his followers on the voyage—Te Kooti from the outset was more implicitly obeyed than the high-born chiefs of other tribes, though himself of inferior birth.

Major Biggs, when he found himself unable to induce the ex-prisoners to surrender, sent to Napier for assistance, and raised such a force of Europeans and friendly natives at Turanga as was possible. This body, eighty-eight in all, was commanded by Captain Westrup, and was fully armed and equipped. Te Kooti, who had made no secret of his intention to make for the Uriwera Mountains first and then to return and destroy Turanga, at length began his march. Unfortunately, Major Biggs and Captain Westrup resolved to intercept him with their mixed force without waiting for reinforcements or instructions from the government.

The result was that on July 20th, at a point in the bush some miles up the Arai Valley called Paparatu, Captain Westrup was attacked in the most spirited manner by Te Kooti, and completely defeated with the loss of his camp, stores, horses, reserve ammunition, and many of his arms, and was compelled to make a precipitate retreat. His loss had only comprised two killed and seven wounded, but the effect had been disastrously demoralising to his force and proportionately encouraging to the returned prisoners, who attributed this, the most utter rout of the Pakeha which had ever occurred, to Te Kooti's supernatural power. Undoubtedly the extraordinary prestige this remarkable man afterwards acquired, sprang from this brilliant and to the Maori mind inexplicable success.

Such was the opening of the East Coast and Uriwera Campaign of 1868-9, and, as in most British warlike operations, it began with a reverse as unlooked for as unaccountable. Already on the West Coast war had commenced in equal gloom, and the surprise of Turu-Turu-Mokai, though by no means an equal military disaster, had been a more bloody success of the insurgent Maoris. But Paparatu was destined to be the first act of a tragedy of which the massacre of Poverty Bay and the atonement of Ngatapa were to be the closing scenes, and it is not hard to trace how entirely the blood shed at the massacre was due to the misadventure to our arms at the skirmish of July 20th.

On the 21st about twenty Europeans and forty native volunteers under my command, arrived in the bay, to be followed by the 1st division of the A. C. from Opotiki, under Major Fraser. A special steamer had been sent to bring this reinforcement, but the weather was so boisterous that its arrival was delayed. Directly we landed we marched to reinforce Captain Westrup, but on reaching the entrance to the Arai valley we met the leading fugitives, and of course received exaggerated reports of the disaster. Proceeding onwards at last we met the main body and then the rear guard, who had saved the lives, if it could not save the credit, of the rest; the true details which we now obtained were highly honourable to Captain Westrup, and the small band which had borne the brunt in the engagement and protected the rear in retreat.

It is not necessary to record the story. It was a day of shame to our arms, but it illustrated very forcibly the danger of being led away by the apparent eagerness of the men to attempt operations in a New Zealand bush, even under favourable circumstances, with untrained and inexperienced troops. The military disgrace of defeat, and the misfortune of showing ourselves so unfavourably to the Maoris, would have produced a worse effect, however, but for the devotion of the little detachment which rallied round Captain Westrup, and by their constancy and their pluck prevented the rout from becoming a massacre. The Maoris usually value a success by the number of the slain, and on this occasion their trophies in that respect were, thanks to Captain Westrup's rear guard, exceedingly small, though in other respects as estimated by a European standard, significant enough.

As soon as the force had been collected and obtained a little rest, in the Arai valley, I had the men assembled and endeavoured to induce them to renew operations next day. Encumbered as he was, Te Kooti could not move rapidly, and I hoped to overtake him at no great distance and retrieve the honour of our arms, but nothing could move the great bulk of the force, they were hopelessly dejected after their defeat, and even the hope of recovering the spoils wrested from them by the insurgents had no effect. A few were ready to make the attempt, but their voices were drowned in the general outcry against my proposal. Compromise was equally vain. If not next day, then on what day would they be ready? I asked, with no better success. Failing by entreaty, I at last used reproaches, perhaps unwisely, but as I conscientiously felt that I asked no more than in their places I would readily have done myself, I felt much disgusted with their refusal.

In the end I gave it up, and resolved to hold the ground with my twenty or thirty Europeans and Maori volunteers till joined by Major Fraser and his division of the armed Constabulary. By the next morning it was evident that, except that part of Captain Westrup's force which had already done so much, I could not rely on any local aid for some time to come, and it would have been impossible after so much time had been lost to undertake a pursuit without, at all events, sufficient men both to fight and to keep up a supply of provisions.

A great deal was made of the terms I used under feelings of considerable exasperation in stigmatizing the conduct of the Poverty Bay men. It was impolitic, and my language may have been ill-chosen to men so dispirited as those I addressed, but with my gallant friends Col. Herrick, Captain Carr, and Mr. Davis Canning, I had left my home gratuitously on purpose to aid fellow settlers in their difficulties, and we had done this out of the purest motives of goodwill to settlers of our own race, most of them strangers to us and inhabiting a district in which not one of us had the smallest interest whatever. Not until every effort to restore their courage had failed, not until every reasonable compromise had been rejected, not until replies which ill became them had been made by some, did I suffer myself to utter one word of reproach or show the smallest lack of sympathy with their misfortunes.

But though primarily interested, they were members of the European community subject to the duty of repressing disturbances if called upon by authority, and they had the same and even greater risk to run if they allowed a Maori insurgent force to get clear away with the trophies and the prestige of an unexampled success. I certainly regret having been betrayed into using language which expressed my feelings of the moment, but I claim that it was neither unreasonable nor undeserved, and though silence might have been wiser, yet that it was hard to maintain it at the time, believing as I did that unless the pursuit began at once Te Kooti would probably escape. I halted until joined by Major Fraser, who was much delayed, and by this time a new force was organised by Major Biggs and Captain Westrup to co-operate.

The Napier volunteers gave me some trouble, refusing to march unless supplied with biscuit which was unprocurable, and rejecting the flour ration which was the only possible substitute. My actual powers were so small that had they been known I could not in such an undisciplined force have maintained order at all, but luckily nobody seemed to be aware that I had no more power to punish than a subaltern on detachment. Consequently, I had to set the solemn farce of trying the ringleaders by detachment general court martial for mutiny. It was essential to produce an impression that might ensure subordination, and desirable to get it done before the Poverty Bay contingent arrived. I well knew that at that season and in the country before me great hardships must be endured, and it would have been hopeless to attempt to move if my orders were regarded as admitting of argument.

Consequently, I explained to Major Fraser, the President, that while it was essential to keep up serious appearances, the court must find the prisoners guilty of mutinous conduct only, in order that the highest punishment which could really be given might be awarded without letting out the secret of my powerlessness. Much amusement to those who were behind the scenes, was afforded by what followed. The ringleaders when selected, behaved in the most craven manner, making the most piteous entreaties to be spared: "I am no ringleader, sir, for the love of God, let me off, sir. Sentry, as you are a Christian give me a start of six yards, do," and so on, were the appeals they interjected, while the court was sitting, and the President writing the minutes on an old biscuit-box which did duty as a drum.

At each outcry silence was ordered in loud tones, and to improve the occasion, I asked, incidentally, "Sergeant-Major, are those men ready with the spades?" which produced another wail from the prisoners who heard me. At last the mockery came to an end, the proceedings were brought for my approval which I attached, and then read them aloud. I improved the occasion by telling the prisoners that the court had taken a very merciful view of their offence, and that they had had a very narrow escape. They were then dismissed with ignominy, a bugler beating an old can down the ranks behind them, and they were marched under an escort to the steamer to undergo at Napier the short imprisonment which was the highest sentence any court convened by me could award, or I confirm.

This really ridiculous incident answered its object and sufficed to create a belief that I had powers as great as an officer in the service similarly situated would have held, and was likely to use them. When Parliament met the case was provided for by legislation, and the Governor was empowered to issue warrants to colonial officers which up to that period had always been granted by the general commanding H. M.'s troops, alone. The garbled versions of the story which got about were most amusing, and at Poverty Bay, when I reached that place some months after, the walls were decorated with placards announcing that the "grave-digger had arrived."

Te Kooti's line of retreat lay in a southerly direction across the high range, called Ahi-manu, running parallel to the coast, to an open plain called Waihau, in which several large lakes are situated. This point is more or less due west of Wairoa, and as Major Biggs had sent notice of what had occurred to the resident magistrates and the several loyal chiefs of that district, a considerable force of friendly Maoris and a few Europeans were collected to aid the settlers of Poverty Bay against Te Kooti. This force was under Captain Richardson, A.C., and Captain Greece, N.Z.M., and it marched by the Waihau lakes towards Turanga. It had not, however, got much beyond Waihau when, on July 24th, it was met by Captain Wilson with despatches from me, directing Captain Richardson to return to Waihau and endeavour to intercept Te Kooti, or at least to impede his progress until my force could come up.

It seems that the Wairoa natives had already shown some symptoms of faint-heartedness, and that at least one small *hapu* was disaffected. The return march was a disappointment, as the friendlies had begun to look forward to a pleasant week or two's feasting at Turanga. However, Captain Richardson retired as directed, and took post at the head of the valley leading to Wairoa on the Konaki ridge. Before dark Te Kooti's column of march came in sight with its horses, women, and children. Probably Captain Richardson's force was under 150 men, but only eighteen were Europeans, and the natives were of little account. Te Kooti lost no time in attacking, and very soon after the whole of the friendlies, except four, deserted and made off towards Wairoa.

Captain Richardson kept up the unequal fight, nobly seconded by Captain Preece and a few Europeans, until as night closed in, he was compelled to withdraw under cover of darkness. Unfortunately, there was no telegraph in those days, or Te Kooti might easily have been stopped, if not altogether defeated, by a proper force at Waihau. But it has always proved to be the case that where the friendlies constitute the great bulk of the force, it is impossible to rely on any satisfactory results. On this occasion it was worse because by their conduct they nearly caused the destruction of the Europeans with them, and imperilled the safety of the Wairoa settlement.

Te Kooti's success at Waihau over the Maori force was, to the Mao-

CAPTAIN G. MAIR, N.Z.C.

COLONEL PORTER, C.B.

CAPTAIN G. PREECE, N.Z.C.

ri mind, a signal victory and a brilliant feat of arms. He rested a few days upon his laurels, obtaining accessions to his force from the ranks of the Wairoa natives who were secretly disaffected. Of these the most prominent was Rakoroa, a petty chief, who had been recently armed and equipped with the rest of his *hapu*, and who now deserted with his whole following to Te Kooti. While halted at Hangaroa ford close to Waihau, Te Kooti intercepted one of my messengers, a half-caste of good birth, Paku Brown by name, and had him shot in cold blood, killing his dog at the same time, and throwing it on the body to insult the dead.

Chapter 2

Te Kooti Escaped at Ruaki-Ture

It was July 31st before I could get fully started from Poverty Bay upon Te Kooti's trail. I had to encounter great difficulties. The weather had been most unfavourable, the rain had flooded the rivers, and I had to improvise a commissariat supply, but I did not allow any of these things to delay me, and moved off directly Major Fraser's reinforcements arrived. I myself, with part of the force, took the direct line by which Te Kooti had marched, but sent the Poverty Bay contingent by the better and easier track to Waihau. It was a service of endurance; two nights we camped in snow, our men consumed their supplies for four days easily in two, and when I offered a few of the Napier volunteers—who were without rations, or even fuel, for they had thrown away the axes I had issued them—an extra allowance of flour, I did so with affected diffidence "because you fellows don't care for flour." "Try us, sir," was the answer. It is, perhaps, unnecessary to say that when I did, no time was lost in converting it into dampers.

I started from Poverty Bay with a little more than 200 men; half, or thereabouts, consisted of the Napier division A. C. Napier volunteers and Napier natives, in all 118 men; and Turanga natives, Coast natives, and Turanga volunteers to about the same numbers. On August 3rd, after a toilsome march and great obstruction from rain and snow, the two columns united at Waihau. On the 5th the entire force reached Hangaroa River bank, having passed on the march the *kainga* where poor Paku Brown had been shot; the sight of the dead body produced on the friendlies from Poverty Bay a depressing effect, as he was a person of consequence among them, and it was, therefore, easy for the European volunteers from Turanga to induce them to fall into their views which they then communicated to me. We had seen Te Kooti's watch-fires, and knew he was not far ahead.

Hard work and hard knocks were clearly before us, and the Turanga men resolved to leave us from Napier to encounter both alone. They told me they had reached the limits of their district, a ludicrous excuse to make to us, who had left our own district to aid them. But I had had some experience already of these volunteers, and I knew how useless it was to urge the ordinary arguments advanced on such occasions, so I suffered them to go in peace, even ordering them back, ostensibly to keep up the supply of provisions by pack animals. I did not forget what Henry V. said before Agincourt, that "he who has no stomach for the fight, let him depart," and away they went with their store of rations, and the boots, blankets, and equipments issued to enable them to carry out the expedition.

It was, however, disheartening, for it was evident that their numbers might have just turned the scale if Te Kooti made vigorous resistance; and, as it turned out, even a portion of their rations, had they left them behind, would have altered the results of the next few days' operations. It is, however, fair to state that a few of them, among whom was the only doctor with the force, Dr. Brown, declined to abandon us. I left these men, except the doctor, who gallantly acquitted himself later on, to take charge of our horses and all impedimenta with which we could dispense, at a sort of camp at the head of the valley leading to the Wairoa, near the scene of Captain Richardson's engagement.

The plain duty of a commanding officer in my position was to push on, unless the odds against me were hopelessly great. As regards the enemy's actual armed force I did not believe that we were outnumbered, notwithstanding the uncertainty existing as to the number of recruits he might have attracted to his ranks, but there were other difficulties even more serious than the numerical force against us, for if we could overtake Te Kooti in the open I had no doubt of easily defeating him; but the winter season was at its worst, and the rivers were flooded; we were in high country, and had had to bivouac two nights already in the snow, which our native force had felt very much.

We could hardly rely very confidently upon the loyalty of the Poverty Bay force to insure our being supplied with provisions by pack transport, and in addition to the unknown but certain hardships and difficulties of the country before us, and the risks of the weather, the prospect of starvation was by no means enlivening to the Napier men.

But, as I have seen on many occasions, the spirit of the Hawke's Bay settlers, most of whom have been inured to hard work and privation on the hill-sheep runs of the Province, rose as the difficulties before them increased, and not one man flinched from his duty; nay, more, their spirit was caught by the native allies from Napier, and they, too, disdained to follow the example of their relatives and friends from the coast. To complicate my personal difficulty in deciding what course to pursue, I now received a despatch from Captain Richardson from the Wairoa, informing me that Mr. Locke, a gentleman often confidentially employed by the government in native matters, in passing Wairoa, had stated that despatches were on the way to me recalling the expedition.

I reflected over all the features of the case, and balanced all the arguments that occurred to me on both sides as I lay awake all night, but I could find no justification for turning aside, at all events till I had done my utmost to overtake Te Kooti. The reported recall of the force was, after all, only hearsay, and ultimately proved unfounded.

Accordingly, on the morning of the 6th, leaving whatever we could not carry, we crossed the Hangaroa in canoes. We were 118 of all ranks, 76 being Europeans, 42 natives, and the two chiefs Hotane and Te Poro from Poverty Bay, who elected to leave their tribe and accompany us. We were rationed only to the night of the 8th, and, failing the arrival of pack horses by another route, we should after that evening be without food, unless we could find potatoes, or overtake Te Kooti and supply ourselves from his store. I made as light as I could of the defections from our ranks so as not to discourage those who stood to their colours, but it was hardly necessary to take any pains in this direction, so excellent was the disposition and so high the spirits of the men.

We pushed on through the fern as fast as we could, keeping the trail of the enemy which was clearly defined, and by nightfall we had reached Te Kooti's camp of the 4th, the fires of which we had seen from Waihau. Husbanding our rations as best we could, we marched again early on the 7th, pushing forward with all possible speed, passing Te Kooti's camp of the 5th, and at sunset reaching his camp of the 6th and sleeping there. The enemy had not left us much to get by foraging, for his rear-guard had not long left the ground, but one or two small pigs and a few seed potatoes were obtained from a *kainga* not far off, to assuage the pangs of hunger, for the rations had already been consumed. We were now unfortunately at the edge of the bush, and as our rations were more than exhausted, I felt that I could, without dishonour, turn back and claim to have done all that was possible, but the men themselves were desirous to make another effort, and I was glad to encourage their spirit.

Leaving therefore our blankets and empty haversacks, so as to march light, and directing the guard left in charge to shoot and cook a stray colt we had caught, we moved off early by a well-defined track through the bush. By this time, as hunting men would say, the scent was burning hot; we could see, at every step, indications that the enemy had but recently passed. Twigs broken, probably by those in front to mark the track, were still fresh, and every few minutes we heard, not far ahead, the shots of their pigeon shooters echoing along the valley through the forests.

We found also several messages written on the bark of trees, evidently quite fresh, one of which stated that the ex-prisoners meant to make their way eventually to Ahi-Kereru, a settlement on the western side of the Uriwera country at a spot sometimes called Te Whaiti. At first these messages suggested a possibility of a detachment of Te Kooti's force being behind us, perhaps being sent towards the Upper Wairoa for recruiting purposes, but I concluded that any detachment shortly expected to return would not have required to know the ultimate destination of Te Kooti, as Ahi-kereru was distant, and encumbered as they were, the ex-prisoners could not reach it for weeks. We therefore hastened on along a hillside overhanging the Ruaki-ture River which we occasionally saw below us, and at length the trail turned down to the bed of the stream and ascended the valley along its banks.

Shot after shot, at short intervals, probably fired at pigeons, proved to us how close we were to the object of our pursuit; at each shot the men pushed forward faster, and became more hopeful. Our advanced guard, led by Mr. Davis Canning, who besides being one of the bravest gentlemen to be met with, was a most excellent bushman, pressed on almost too impetuously, and in each turn in the river all eyes were strained to catch a glimpse of the enemy. It was a fine day, and though the nights were cold, the sun at mid-day was hot, and the men marching on empty stomachs began to suffer from fatigue. At last we came to a spot where Te Kooti had evidently encamped before crossing the stream, the fires being still alight. It was past mid-day, well on to one o'clock, and we halted in the bed of the stream.

The men took this opportunity to remind me respectfully of my promise. No shots had been heard for some time. Hunger and fatigue began to tell on the bravest and the strongest of the force. The river swollen with snow water did not look inviting to cross, and I felt I had at last reached the limit of what was practicable. Reluctantly and regretfully, I had acquiesced in the justice of my men's representations, and in a few minutes more we should have begun to retrace our steps.

My disappointment was I suppose apparent, for Captain Carr, of the Royal Artillery, begged me to allow him to make his way a little further on through the bush upon our side of the river to the next bend in order to reconnoitre, adding the characteristic remark, "And then if I cannot see them we can return, consoling ourselves that we have trailed our coat through the Uriwera country, and nobody has dared to jump upon it." I made no objection, and he disappeared in the bush. In a very short time, he returned bright and cheerful, and the men crowded round to hear his report. Not a hundred yards, he said, beyond the next bend, there appeared to be an island in the river, and at that point the enemy was halted, apparently awaiting us. The distance was not great, perhaps four or five hundred yards in all, and no very great obstacle seemed to intervene. This intelligence changed the aspect of affairs.

The men, anxious before to return, now besought me to lead them on. I waited long enough to satisfy myself whether the enthusiasm was genuine, but when it was clearly the wish of the force to release me from my promise, the advance was ordered, and we plunged into the ford. The water was cruelly cold, at all points up to our waists, and in some spots deeper. To keep our powder dry, the men fastened their pouches round their necks and slung their carbines muzzle downwards. The force of the stream was such that they had to form a sort of chain, six or eight holding hands to steady themselves against the stream, and to prevent falling over the boulder stones of the bed. We found that we had to cross two or three times in all before we reached the next bend where the enemy opened fire directly, we came in sight.

Taking cover behind some immense rocks until they had put themselves into trim, and had overcome the shivering and teeth-chattering caused by the coldness of the water, the men in a few minutes advanced resolutely to the attack. Captain Herrick, however, with the Maoris, I had directed to re-cross the river to take the enemy on the island in flank and reverse. I cannot say Captain Herrick was very well seconded in his efforts by his men.

The white volunteers were not trained soldiers and set a bad example to the Maori volunteers, but some of each force did fairly well, and several most gallantly. An old chief from Napier, Paul Kaiwhata, got into position behind a rock in the bed of the stream and fired away as fast as he could load, though recognised by the ex-prisoners who

Scene of Ruakiture fight

knew him well, and addressed him by name. Captain Herrick, with a portion of his force, at length gained the position assigned to him, and fired upon Te Kooti's right rear. Upon this I directed the advance guard to move on, and unfortunately Captain Carr and Mr. Canning went with it. I had not regained the front of the column, as the scramble along the river bed was difficult, and I had been obliged to go back to despatch Captain Herrick's force to make the movement I have described.

By the time I did reach the spot the advance guard had been driven back with the loss of both Captain Carr and Mr. Canning. The former suffering from the infirmity of deafness, had not in all probability heard the voices of the advance guard calling them back, and thus fallen among the enemy. Mr. Canning was, however, shot dead leading the men. I at once pushed on again and recovered the ground, though unhappily we could not find Mr. Canning's body. The enemy were now retiring, and in so dense a bush we could no longer see distinctly as the winter evening was closing in. There was nothing for it therefore but to return. We had no food and several wounded.

If there was a road or any dry spot to encamp, we could not see to find it; so, I had to draw off the men before the twilight changed to dark. Luckily Te Kooti himself had been wounded, and had experienced losses heavier than our own. He had been driven from the island, and was in full retreat towards Puketapu, a mountain in the Uriwera country, at the foot of which the action was fought. Had we had another hour's daylight we should probably have turned his retreat into a flight and captured some of his pack horses with provisions.

As it was, we had to return ignorant of his condition, and only guessing it by the fact that no attempt whatever was made, except a few desultory shots, probably from a few men left as a rear-guard, to molest us as we retired. We bore off our wounded, however, getting them across the river with the greatest possible difficulty. We were wholly unable to carry away the dead. No one knew in what direction poor Captain Carr had fallen, and our search for Mr. Canning had been unsuccessful. We knew him to be dead, as he had fallen with the advance guard, and had even sent back his revolver and carbine to me with the message that he had died doing his duty.

It took sixteen men, eight on each side, to steady each bearer of a wounded man in crossing the river, and the few remaining of our force were required to protect the rear from attack, if it should be attempted. It was a great effort of endurance marching back to our blankets with the wounded through the night. The natives did not assist in this labour, but they provided a huge fire to dry the men after they had crossed the river for the last time.

All the night our men toiled up the hill, carrying the wounded, a hill so easy to descend in daylight and in high spirits, but at night with the groans of several seriously wounded men ringing in their ears, after the reaction from great excitement had set in, when hunger began to press upon them, and the hard frost of the Uriwera country chilled them to the marrow of their bones, the long ascent at a snail's pace was trying and painful to a degree. It was mid-day before we reached the blankets. In ten minutes, the cooked colt was devoured by the ravenous men, and the bleeding shank bones were struggled for to complete the meal. At 4 p.m., I ordered the force to march, and by that time a few hours' rest had restored the strength so much tried in the twenty-nine hours of the previous day. Happily, Mr. Gascoigne had not failed us, and by marching two hours back towards the Hangaroa, the men were enabled to obtain a decent meal.

The indecisive engagement of the Ruaki-ture undoubtedly tempered the triumph with which Te Kooti presented himself to the Uriwera; wounded, with a considerable loss, he had not quite the prestige which after Paparatu and Waihau he had gained. It was all we could do, and it had a certain moral effect, hardly worth the cost of so many valuable lives to a superficial critic, but to the Maori mind a great deal nevertheless. To us who had come in brotherhood to help our fellow-countrymen of Poverty Bay, it was grievous to think, that what we, by ourselves, could only partially perform, must have been decisively successful had we had the assistance of the men whom we had gone so far and risked our lives to help.

But it had been a feat of human endurance as well as of ordinary "pluck" such as the Colonial force had never before accomplished. To this day those who underwent the hardships and privations of those few days are wont to talk of them as Arctic travellers do of their more painful trials. Hardly as we Colonial troops can expect to meet with sympathy or encouragement in a colony as yet too young to possess a national spirit, still it was with disgust even more than disappointment that our men found that the trade of politics had so influenced the leading professors of the art in the colony, that no credit was given to them for their exertions, and that the honour which was their due was withheld by those who opposed the government.

The massacre three months later of those they knew best, and, alas!

many helpless ones whom they loved, was the direct consequence of the conduct of the Poverty Bay men, and doubtless they have regretted it since. We at the moment were sorrowing over the untimely death of our two gallant friends, Captain Carr and Mr. Canning, and felt very bitter, and could see no justification for the treatment we had experienced.

CHAPTER 3

Opening of the West Coast Campaign

My share of the operations under Lieut.-Colonel McDonnell was of no importance, not worth mentioning in itself, but such as it was it tended to give that officer a moral and military support which he much needed at the time.

I had returned from Patea and had resumed my seat in the Legislative Council, and was doing what I could to support the government in taking effectual steps to reinforce the troops, when one evening, early in October, I was unexpectedly sent for to his quarters by Colonel Haultain, the Defence Minister. I found Mr. Booth, the resident magistrate from Patea, with him, who was the bearer of the resignation of his command by Lieut.-Colonel McDonnell, on family grounds which were well understood and very sad. With his resignation he sent to the Ministry a suggestion that the command should be offered to me, and Colonel Haultain, in the name of the Cabinet, offered it to me accordingly.

At that time, I was a member of the Legislative Council, who, though professedly on the side of those who were opposed to the continuance of all the powers of the provinces, and therefore recognised Mr. Stafford in a general way as our leader, still had never taken any strong part on either side.

I was also engaged in managing a considerable fern run, and in the serious struggle of reclaiming a large area of wilderness and making it suitable for sheep. Times were bad, and sheep farmers had much to do to keep afloat, with prices such as wool was producing. It had never occurred to me that I might be asked to serve continuously in the regular Colonial Force, or if it had I should have dismissed any such notion, as I could not afford to do so. But now, when affairs seemed so critical, I doubted if I had a right to refuse to serve, temporarily at

51

MAJOR MAIR, N.Z.M.

SIR EDWARD WILLIAM STAFFORD, G.C.M.G.

LIEUT.-COL. NOAKE, N.Z.M.

least. I therefore asked for a day or so to consider. Colonel Haultain accorded this to me, and I consulted the late Sir J. Richardson and several old Imperial officers, of whom, in those days, there were many in Parliament.

I placed myself unreservedly in their hands, in order to ascertain what seemed to them my duty. They all replied in the same sense, that unless it meant positive ruin to my affairs, I was bound to serve at least till the crisis was past. I had still a doubt whether I could assume the command, for I had no other relation in the country on whom I could rely in case of accident to myself, and my wife was in New Zealand. In such an event she would have been friendless or dependent upon strangers. I therefore resolved to consult her before accepting the risk, and left for Napier with this object. But though it was hard upon her, my wife recognised that I must not evade my duty, and admitted that those I had consulted had decided rightly. I therefore made what arrangements at short notice I could and returned to Wellington.

The fact of my acceptance of the command, or perhaps, more correctly, that of Lieut.-Colonel McDonnell's retirement, restored to Mr. Stafford enough of his erring partisans to secure a substantial majority to the end of the Session, which was therefore speedily brought to a close.

I reached Wanganui on October 20th, 1868, on my way to Patea, and endeavoured to ascertain the position of affairs. Very much to my surprise, Lieut.-Colonel McDonnell did not come to see me, or afford me the least assistance. But there were many who were well-informed and I soon got to know very fairly the position of affairs. It was a serious one. Titokowaru, flushed with success, had moved forward to a hill not far from and overlooking Patea, called "Gentle Annie." The last advanced post beyond Patea itself (Kakaramea) had been abandoned, and of open country round the township we held not a rood.

The enemy, at the outbreak of hostilities but seventy strong, had, as he moved forward, been joined successively by the Tangahoe and Papakohe *hapus*, and by many restless spirits from the Taranaki and Waikato tribes. Secret negotiations were believed to be in progress with the Ngarauru or Waitotara *hapu*, the most numerous of the Ngatiruanui sub-tribes, which threatened a still more considerable accession to the numbers in rebellion.

All these *hapus* were more or less, but the Ngarauru were very closely connected with the loyal Wanganuis, so that there was a danger of the whole of the West Coast tribes making common cause against

53

the government, and joining the standard of Titokowaru. To oppose the force openly in rebellion, and any further possible accessions to his ranks which seemed dangerously likely to follow before long, we had but a miserable excuse for a military force. At Patea we had, after the troops had fallen back upon it, in consequence of the defeat of Te Ngutu, the remnants of Nos. 2 and 3 divisions of A. C., and the intact division from Napier No. 1, about fifty strong. No. 5 (Von Tempsky's) division had mutinied, and were disbanded; so that there were but between seventy and eighty men fit for service in the whole three divisions at Patea, and of these some were occupied with the care of the wounded.

There were also the fragments of the hurriedly-raised, and for the most part, wholly untrained levies from Patea and Wellington, Taranaki, and Nelson. These were reduced by casualties and desertions, and their term of service was almost expired. The Taranaki and Nelson little corps were probably the most valuable of these, and might have been, or part might have been, induced to renew their period of service in the field. But the rest, the Wellington volunteers more especially, who had but a few days to serve, positively refused to remain a day longer than compelled by their engagement. There was no possibility of forcing these men to remain or continue to serve, and when they withdrew the force at Patea would be barely sufficient to hold the town and guard the hospital, magazines, and stores.

To supplement the field force a body of 400 of the Wanganui tribe, including the old, the young, the weak, and the cowardly, had been hastily ordered up, and had gradually collected at Weraroa, where there were a few recruits of the armed constabulary lately sent up to be trained. This post, a mile or two to the right of the line of communication at Nukumaru, was itself accessible to wheel traffic by a road along a ridge close to a dense bush, but the track went no further. It was situated on the south of the Waitotara River at a spot which overhung that stream. It was most undesirable to permit the congregation of Wanganuis at Weraroa.

Their relationship to the Ngarauru, whose loyalty was more than suspected, made it imprudent to allow them to remain in the immediate vicinity of the villages of that *hapu*—but up to this all effort to induce them to move on to Patea had failed. Situated as the colony then was, it would have been disastrous if a large section of the Wanganuis already much impressed by Titokowaru's successes had deserted with the arms and ammunition we had placed in their hands. Te Keepa—

Kemp (as he is more commonly called)—and his immediate followers, comprising less than a quarter of the whole of this native multitude, alone could be absolutely depended upon.

The white population of Wanganui and the country districts adjacent had but two volunteer corps, both cavalry ones, under arms. One, and the larger one, was under Captain Finnimore, and had its headquarters in Wanganui itself, whilst a lesser, but very valuable one under Lieutenant Bryce, was composed of the actual residents of the neighbouring districts. There was no militia.

On taking command I had formally intimated to the ministers my entire want of confidence in the Wanganui native gathering, the little use I thought they would be to me, and the distrust I felt in their loyalty. To this could only be replied that I must do my best with them till the government could procure more reliable troops. Having taken a day to consider such information as I could get, I resolved to proceed at once to Weraroa and endeavour to get these doubtful allies to move forward. On October 31st, accordingly, I left Wanganui and rode to Weraroa with a small escort of the Wanganui cavalry, commanded as it happened by Corporal John Ballance, till recently a cornet in the corps.

The Defence Minister had summarily dismissed this gentleman and cancelled his commission on account of an article, more or less hostile to the government, which had appeared in a newspaper of which he was the proprietor. I do not propose here to go into the merits of this case, but may mention that Mr. Ballance, who has since filled some space in the political history of the colony, did not on account of the punishment inflicted upon him suffer himself to be behind-hand in the duty of defending his district, but re-enlisted in the ranks of his corps and continued to take part in its military duties, till its services were no longer required.

An acquaintance thus formed ripened into a friendship of years. At Weraroa, with the able assistance of Mr. Booth, R.M., I was able to persuade the Wanganui's to march forward next day, and received satisfactory promises of good behaviour from all the chiefs. I then proceeded to Patea. In point of fact my command only extended northwards from the Whenuakura River, but being the senior officer Lieut.-Colonel Gorton who commanded at Wanganui, made no objection to my exercising control over Wairoa (now called Waverley) and Weraroa which were actually in his district, though held by my force.

At Patea I found the whole population of the district and all the stock crammed into the small intervening space between the town, the river, and the sea. It appeared that all had lost heart, and their tone resembled that of men when in a shipwreck; all hope had been abandoned. In order therefore to make at least a show of more confidence, I lost no time in moving the whole force from the township and establishing my headquarters at Mr. Booth's house, three-quarters of a mile in advance. There I encamped, stretching a line of tents from the river to the sea sand-hills. This step had at least the advantage of giving elbow-room, and space for the stock. It also made a demonstration easily seen from the enemy's position, and it removed the men from the nightly orgies which of late had been too common in the town. The guard left that night in Patea nearly all got drunk, two of the men next morning were found to be seriously stabbed, and twenty-one prisoners, all of whom had been on duty, with several others were paraded at my headquarters next day.

Such a state of things made strong measures unavoidable. Therefore, I at once appointed a Provost Marshal with large powers of summary punishment, and told off a picquet of a few mounted troopers to prevent all intercourse between the township and camp. A canteen under strict regulations was opened, and under powers vested in me by recent legislation I closed the other public houses for the sale of liquor. These steps secured sobriety in the force, and prevented a bad example being shown to the native auxiliaries hourly expected. These latter arrived in the evening, and at once made me feel how pitiable a position it was to be dependent to any extent upon them. The spot fixed for their camp did not suit them and they declined to encamp there. Native dissatisfaction is always rather loudly expressed, and this was my first attempt to manage Maori allies. The difficulty was, however, at last got over practically by giving in to their claim, and they settled down.

The repression of drunkenness, which had been rather neglected hitherto in the Patea force, was, however, but an essential preliminary to the task of making the men efficient and creating a military spirit among them. Discipline and training had not been sufficiently attended to before Te Ngutu, and after that disaster it had become difficult to find time to inculcate discipline or to train the men. Nevertheless, it did not admit of delay if the men were to fight, and I felt that I must act in some way at once or Titokowaru would neglect my force and invade the settled districts. I had already made a sort of demonstration by pitching tents to induce a belief that we had been reinforced, and I resolved to draw out the whole of the troops and the Wanganui natives, as a reconnaissance in force, to prove to the enemy that the tents were not unoccupied.

One day I had to occupy in completing the camp arrangements at Patea, and erecting a central redoubt and open works on the flanks of my position, and then on Sunday the 25th, I marched with all my available force and the native contingent under their chiefs and Mr. Gudgeon as their staff officer. The Maoris turned out readily enough, and from their scattered mode of marching made some display of numbers. We got to the ravine intervening between the open country and "Gentle Annie," Titokowaru's camp, which was pitched in deep jungle, and fired a few shells at some 200 to 250 of his men, who showed near the summit of the hill at a distance of about 1200 yards. Nothing more, however, could be done, nor had I intended to do more, as the bush ravine was both heavily wooded and precipitous, and to have gone round the head of it to attack the hill from the rear would have occupied more time than we could devote to the movement. We therefore returned before sunset to our lines.

Next day, the 26th, "Governor" Hunia, a chief with a considerable following, again gave trouble about his camping ground; not that he cared twopence where he encamped, but simply to assert his own importance, and enjoy the impotence of "the Pakeha." Hunia was talked over at last, the more easily that he really had nothing to complain about.

I now decided to pay off and dismiss the Wellington Rifles. I had no means of detaining them, their time was almost up: without a good deal of training they were of no use, and it seemed better to make a merit of necessity. They were therefore informed that they were free to go. I devoted the evening to an interview with the Maori chiefs, which though fairly satisfactory—inasmuch as they declared that they would fight while they remained—gave them an opportunity of telling me they would not long remain at the front, as they required to return home shortly to plant their crops.

On October 27th I received from the government, despatches promising me recruits, approving my bringing up the Wanganui natives, and informing me that, though doing their best, it must be some time before the Maoris could be replaced by reliable Europeans. I sent back the Wellington Rifles by the steamer that brought up my despatches, and ordered out our few mounted men with the natives to patrol the neighbourhood. This duty was cheerfully performed, and the village of Hukatere burned, as the inhabitants had joined Titokowaru.

On the 28th I sent an escort with four carts to supply Wairoa with a month's provisions to prevent the embarrassment of having to send, as hitherto, almost daily supplies. Sub-Inspector Col. McDonnell had now some twenty or thirty recruits at Weraroa to support the fifty Wanganui natives whom I had been compelled to leave there rather against my will. An escort of 200 natives had been ordered to reinforce the escort of the carts to Wairoa, but somehow, they did not appear. This was their first actual instance of disobedience, and promised ill for the future. They endeavoured to put the blame on Mr. Gudgeon, their staff-officer, but it was clearly their own fault, not his.

In the evening I had a further foretaste of what it was to have to rely upon so broken a reed as a tribal collection of Maoris. I had reason to suspect that Titokowaru, if he had not yet moved round my flank by the bush inland, was likely to do so before long, and I therefore proposed at an evening meeting that the tribe should march in the night or early morning to Little Taranaki to reconnoitre.

This village was one which the enemy would probably visit, even though not meaning to hold it, if he undertook the movement I expected. But many hours "*korero*" was wasted. Commands are of no use unless they can be enforced, and the Wanganuis knew well enough I was unable to compel their obedience. Each chief, each reputed soothsayer or wiseacre, had a volume of eloquence to vent in opposition to my plan. The moon was unfavourable, a peculiar star was unpropitious, and so on, and I had to put up with this rodomontade as well as I could. It would have been fatal to lose my temper I knew, because the Maoris often act in this way for no other object than to "raise your dander," and if they fail it is easier to manage them afterwards. So, I accepted the argument of the "star" and deferred the expedition. Next day I took the mounted men myself by Oika to Wairoa and endeavoured to obtain intelligence.

Nothing, however, could be discovered of the enemy. Oika had not been burnt, though plundered by our natives, and our escort had not been molested in re-victualling Wairoa. Such as remained of the Patea temporary volunteers now agreed to serve a little longer, and were brought into our lines. The last of the cattle from Mr. Southwell's farm were brought in under escort of our mounted men to diminish the risks of loss from marauding parties of the enemy. Next day all except a gun detachment of the Nelson and Taranaki temporary volunteers and one or two who enlisted in the A. C., I dismissed to their homes by the steamer *Sturt;* and a clean sweep being then made of all the irregular troops, I wrote urgent despatches to government pressing that in future all recruits should be enrolled in the A. C., and not as temporary volunteers.

On the 31st "Governor" Hunia intimated to me that his men could only stop one week longer, and Kemp, on being referred to, told me regretfully that his men wished to go and could not be relied upon to stop.

On November 1st Kemp and Hunia, with Mr. Gudgeon, moved out in the direction I had wished them to go before, and remained out all night.

On the 2nd, at daylight, a Mr. Kenrich, returning from Wanganui brought me alarming intelligence. He had crossed the Waitotara at its mouth, and there learned that Titokowaru's force had made its way to the river, the Europeans in occupation of native runs only escaping with their lives with difficulty, leaving their stock and effects behind them, and that the Ngarauru (Waitotara tribe) had risen, and joined the enemy. Soon afterwards the native force returned, and informed me that they had visited New Taranaki and Putatahi, and that the enemy on his march had visited those villages, and was probably now moving on Wanganui.

CHAPTER 4

The Reverse at Moturoa

I at once made up my mind to transfer my headquarters with all the available A. C. (70), and such Patea volunteers as I still had, to Wairoa, and endeavour to prevent Titokowaru's incursion into the settled districts beyond the Waitotara. I felt sure the government would approve my action, though I technically left the district over which my command extended. If the Ngarauru had joined I knew Titokowaru's force must be largely increased, probably to 500 or 600 at least, so to approach equality in numbers I must rely on the friendly natives. Therefore, they were ordered to Wairoa, and a section under Hunia obeyed, and followed the little column of Europeans sent in advance to Wairoa. But the bulk of the Wanganuis marched down the coast to the Waitotara mouth. This was not ascertained till evening, and happily at the same time intelligence reached me that a new recruit division from Auckland had disembarked at Wanganui, and was on its march to join the Field Force.

I now examined Captain Hawes, who commanded the settlers at Wairoa, who had enrolled themselves as militiamen, and erected a strong redoubt. His force, about sixty of all kinds, had not been idle under him. He had patrolled the whole of the surrounding country, and the day before Titokowaru's arrival had visited Moturoa, a clearing in the bush at the foot of the Okotuku hill, where we had vaguely learned the enemy was now encamped. Captain Hawes readily agreed to bring some of his men, and to guide a column to Moturoa, where he assured me there was no kind of fortification, only a day or two before. I saw that in that case the sooner we attacked the less probability there would be of a *pah* being erected, or at least completed, and therefore the more hopeful my chances.

Consequently, I resolved to move before daybreak, and endeavour to engage Titokowaru before his fortifications were ready. No. 6 came up late in the afternoon, and a very fine body of young men they were. The commanding officer, Captain Roberts, favourably impressed me, and I was delighted to find the men eager to go into action next day, though just arrived from a long march and sea voyage. They were rather a young average of men, and I thought it best to take out of the ranks those who appeared the weakest and youngest, and to leave them in the redoubt to take the place of the Wairoa settlers, who, to the number of about forty, were to accompany the expedition. I now gave out orders for the march, a little after midnight, of all the troops except No. 6, giving that division an hour or two's more rest. When all were told, the European available force, including the Waverley (Wairoa) settlers, was about 190 strong. During the evening and through the night the Wanganuis held high "*korero*." Unhappily, besides the enemy in front, we had a worse enemy in rear.

There were persons so unpatriotic, and so vile, as in this extremity to be willing to obstruct, to hamper and intrigue, solely to gratify political or personal hostility to the government and to myself. I was, in truth, unknown to these snakes in the grass. What my personal offence was I do not to this day know, but that from the hour I assumed command to the day that I sailed for Auckland, leaving the West Coast, freed from the rebel occupation that I found it in, and reposing in a peace which has ever since been unbroken, I was opposed pertinaciously, insubordination preached to my men, and my smallest action criticised with relentless spite, if not contorted and misrepresented.

My first experience of this was what occurred this night. I had no confidence in the horde of friendly natives under my orders. The composition of the body was at variance with all military organisation. Orders were regarded as themes for discussion, and obeyed or not, as seemed fit.

During the night of the 6th and 7th certain Europeans, whose names I know but do not care at this distant time to specify, came to my camp. The "opposition" at Wanganui had been annoyed at my success in inducing the native force to move up to Patea. It was still more irritated to find that they appeared to get on well with me. It became, in consequence, important to them to prevent my utilising their services. Certain deputies accordingly came up after dark to Wairoa, and attended the native *korero*, employing all their influence to dissuade the tribe from taking an effective part in the anticipated action next day, using freely the names of Messrs. Fox and McLean. I learned from

Te Keepa (as much as he chose then to tell me) that mischief had been rife among his people. I was also informed to the same effect by some Europeans of undeniable reliability and experience, who warned me that the natives might, or some might, prove of no use or treacherous.

This was in no way a matter of surprise, though it certainly did astonish me to hear that my own countrymen, whom I had disobeyed orders to protect, and for whom I was about to engage in a very unequal struggle, should have been base enough to stab me thus in the dark. I hope their patrons did not know, and would not have approved the full turpitude of their action, though done in their name.

The night proved to be dark and showery. For the first time the men had been deliberately made to encamp, or rather bivouac, without tents, at a place where tents might have been brought. But I had told the government, on taking command, that all impedimenta must be abandoned directly I was able to move at all, and that the force must march as in my early days we marched in South Africa. The spirit ration, too, we had dropped, and it is possible that there may have been some friction caused by these sudden changes. Not, however, among the men. These from that day forward never once complained of the hardships and privations it was their fate to suffer under my command. All saw its necessity. All knew I suffered the same myself, and all cheerfully responded to a tax upon their endurance and discipline which they recognised to be unavoidable.

We marched then with all our Patea A. C. and part of Captain Hawes' militia volunteers from Wairoa towards Okotuku at midnight. Night marches are always dreary and more or less dispiriting, but the Europeans showed no lack of willingness. At daylight, or near it, I halted outside of the bush and directed Captain Hawes to employ his militia—who being all actual settlers in the district, and mostly married, I did not wish to use in the bush—in throwing up a small earthwork as a protection if we had to retire, and to form a reserve to guard the ammunition.

No. 6, Roberts' Division, and about fifty Wanganui natives under Te Keepa joined me as day broke. We unloaded our men, leaving their blankets and haversacks at the earthwork Captain Hawes was erecting, and then moved on. The road entered the bush by a cleared path some twelve feet broad and led up to a *pah* which had been erected during the last two days and nights on an open clearing of about 150 yards square. As soon as I came in sight of this work I halted and concealed my men. I then detached No. 1 Division and Kemp's (Te Keepa's) natives to move round by our right, directing them to get close to the *pah* and assail it on that flank while I assaulted it in front. No. 6 I extended on my left. Up to that moment we believed that the work, though apparently complete in the front, could not have been finished in rear, and that our men dashing at the open gorge must be able to penetrate the *pah*. A signal was duly arranged when Kemp and No. 1 should be ready in the bush.

Behind us fifty more natives under Wirihana reached the edge of the bush. The rest, graduated according to their courage or loyalty, were at certain distances along the road sitting down. The great "General Mete Kingi," who was the worst disposed of them all, having got no further than a pistol shot from the Wairoa redoubt where he and the largest section of his tribe squatted to await events.

We in the centre shivering in the raw damp of the morning noticed that no dogs barked, no natives seemed moving to collect wood to light fires which at that hour in the vicinity of any *kainga* or resting-place of Maoris might have been expected, and we called to mind Kemp's remark that he feared they had had warning of our coming. That treachery was afoot among our native allies I have no doubt. They were impressed by Titokowaru's remarkable successes, by the comparative ease with which he had gained possession of so large a district, and by the defection of their relatives the Ngarauru. The sequel shows, that even if not warned the previous evening by the Wanganuis, at least Titokowaru was aware of our approach and fully prepared.

At length the signal was given from our right front, and the storming party under Major Hunter sprang from its concealment and moved rapidly towards the left flank of the *pah* at a double, No. 1 and Kemp's party opening a hot fire on the enemy. Nothing could have been finer than the way in which Major Hunter led his select body of old soldiers. He had his brother killed two months before at Te Ngutu to avenge, he had to vindicate himself from a wanton and most untrue charge of dilatoriness in going to the rescue of the Turu-Turu-Mokai garrison when it was surprised, and no one who saw him that morning could doubt that he would do and dare anything to achieve these objects.

I went with the stormers but, my mind being fully occupied, I forgot in doing so to leave behind a long mackintosh coat I had been wearing. We got close to the angle of the work and Hunter passed on to the rear of it. I stumbled over my coat and fell, and Kemp, thinking me shot, sprang up from behind a log close by to help me. Though within a few yards of the *pah*, however, I was unhurt, and I pushed on to find a weak spot in the palisade. Simultaneously with the advance of the stormers, the enemy had opened fire, the first shot wounding one of our men in the roadway before a single man gained the open clearing. The fire was hotly kept up and replied to by Kemp and No. 1 Division from our right advance. Major Hunter and most of his men got safely past the front of the work, and they were searching for a gate or unfinished spot, when he and two others were hit.

Poor Hunter was shot in the thigh through the femoral artery, and though I tried to staunch the bleeding, the effect of such a wound is so swift, that in less than two minutes he was speechless and beyond human aid. Nevertheless, the three men who supported him stood by him, and though one, if not two, were shot in bearing him out, their places were at once taken by others, and he was eventually carried from the field. I now satisfied myself that short as had been the time, and incredible though it seemed, the *pah* at Moturoa, unlike that at Te Ngutu, was completely closed in and entrance only obtainable by small underground passages.

The palisade, which did not look a formidable one from outside, some months later I was able to examine at my leisure and found to be a double row of stout green timber, with a ditch and bank behind, from which the defenders fired from loopholes or interstices in the palisade almost on the level of the ground. It had by this time become clear, too, that the force and appliances at my command were not sufficient to take a closed-in fortification so strongly held, and that to persevere would only cause a useless waste of life. I therefore directed a deliberate and orderly retreat to cover the removal of such wounded as we already had lost.

The natives under Te Keepa became the first rear-guard, being shortly after replaced by No. 1 Division, which retired through the bush under Captain Goring with great regularity and order. I now sent for No. 6 Division, which, with Captain Roberts at its head, came up at the double in single file, and crossing the rear, knelt down in skirmishing order to allow the other division to withdraw. Te Keepa halted when he regained the roadway with some of his men. No. 6, retiring skirmishing, was now attacked by the enemy almost all along the line, and nearly hand to hand. Through the jungle the deep voice of the gallant commander rang out continually, "Be steady, my men, stick together," and each time a cheery reply, "We will, sir," might have been heard in answer from the "young division." No. 6 retained the name of the "Young Division" which I gave it when it joined me till

MAJOR NORTHCROFT, A.C.

MAJOR SWINDLY, A.C.

LIEUT.-COL. GORING, A.C.

the end of the hostilities.

At one point, so hotly did the enemy press, that one of our men was seized and terribly wounded by tomahawk cuts, so as to present the appearance of a crimped fish. His comrades unluckily devoted their energies to tearing him away from his assailants instead of shooting them down, and though they saved their man, the enemy only lost one of his number at that spot.

The fire of the Terry and Calisher breech-loaders was, however, so hot and well sustained that the enemy ceased to press so heavily on Captain Roberts, and he was thus, after a short time, enabled to extricate his division. Meanwhile I had gone to find Te Keepa, who was searching in and near the roadway for wounded men. In this he seemed to me to expose himself, with utter disregard of danger, and I remonstrated with him to little purpose; for until satisfied that not a wounded man remained, he persisted in examining the ground near where the first fire had reached us.

At last he consented to withdraw, and all the force by degrees, still showing front to the enemy, retired on Captain Hawes' entrenchment. Here I made the men reform their divisions, and commence retiring slowly by fours in column of route. Alternately each division from the front extended, knelt down, and prepared to relieve the rear-guard as it retired skirmishing. As each rear-guard passed its relief, it reformed fours, and rejoined the column. Thus, no rear-guard had to fight more than 150 yards at most, and was sure of support.

I had meanwhile sent to Wairoa for carts to take away the wounded, who were so numerous as to embarrass my small force, for the Maoris did not assist in this duty except in one remarkable instance. The enemy being drawn out at the edge of the bush, fired heavily on the redoubt, where there were still some men loitering in spite of orders, looking for articles they had lost. One of these, a native chief, who chose to expose himself by ostentatiously standing on the parapet calling out defiance to the enemy, was at length shot in the lungs. Few were about, and the rear-guard had passed. I hurried back with Kemp who, seeing no one helping the wounded man, who was a relative of his own, took him in his arms and carried him in safety to the column. The enemy now advanced in a long line of skirmishers, but would not close, nor at the distance he maintained was it possible to do him much injury. I therefore sent for the Armstrong guns to advance from the Wairoa redoubt and take up a position from which they could fire effectively. After we had safely retired something over two miles, and despatched our wounded to Wairoa in the carts, the guns opened on the enemy and fortunately hit off the range at once. This had the desired effect, and drove off his skirmishers, enabling us to resume our march unmolested to Wairoa.

The returns of casualties showed that in this unfortunate engagement we had lost as follows:—

Killed—1 officer, Major Hunter. 4 men.
Wounded—20.
Missing—11; of whom 3 were killed.

It was a very heavy loss and might well have dispirited the force. But the effect on the men was very different. Hardly had I reached Wairoa, when I was requested to see them and begged to resume the attack next day. It was certainly a gratifying proof that their morale was not impaired, and that their spirit was untamed, but hampered as I was with wounded, separated too from supplies, and Patea, where my reserve ammunition and stores were collected, and which was almost without defenders, I could not hesitate what course I should adopt. With wounded it is a recognised principle to move them if possible, to the hospital where they are to remain, before the effect of the shock to the system has worn off.

Therefore, I sent mine under an escort of No. 1 Division in carts to Patea at once, and took steps to fall back behind the Waitotara to be able to keep between Titokowaru and the settlers of Wangnui. I also took away sick women and children as wished to leave under escort of the troops.

New Zealand had no force but mine, small as it was, and the enemy each day gaining strength could, if unopposed, reach Wanganui in two marches. It was true that two companies of H. M.'s 18th Regiment held that town, and with their discipline and training could have kept a host of Maoris at bay. But their orders restricted them to the defensive, and they could not have moved outside of the town. Therefore, if Titokowaru had moved rapidly, all the dwellers in the suburbs must have retreated to the town, and all access to the country and communication by land with me would have been lost. I felt it, therefore, to be my duty, though by doing so I left my district altogether, to cross the Waitotara and place myself between the enemy and my fellow-settlers, trusting to be reinforced either by volunteer militia or by recruits to the constabulary before the enemy, who were not pushing on as fast as his interests should have suggested to him, barred the road to the colony.

I now wrote to the government, placing my resignation in their hands, if in their opinion I had failed to do what was possible at Moturoa, or if the interests of the colony demanded my removal.

With the relics of my force I then crossed the Waitotara and took post at Nukumaru, leaving No. 1 Division and some other men to defend Patea.

The government generously decided to support me in my command. Wanganui at the eleventh hour had responded to the appeal of the officer commanding, and sent me fifty militia to hold the Weraroa redoubt, releasing a few constabulary who were there.

The friendly natives made off to Wanganui, and I strengthened my camp at Nukumaru by an irregular parapet fitted to the ground, rather than to any symmetrical outline.

Patea with No. 1 A. C. and its other defenders was safe from a Maori attack. Wairoa with its redoubt was also safe, and had been recently victualled for a month. Nothing I had found intact had been sacrificed, though the field force had fallen back to Nukumaru to await reinforcements.

To my front was Weraroa—in itself not a valuable position, neither protecting a road or line of communication, nor even forming a post of observation. There were those at Wanganui who exaggerated the importance and prestige of the post. But to me it was simply a drag on my operations, unless at least reliable as an outpost for observation. But Titokowaru had by this time passed the Waitotara himself unseen from it, and had taken post between my camp and the redoubt, and in that position commanded my flank in any movement I made to supply or communicate with the garrison.

I had been promised aid from Wanganui, and that of 1000 nominal militiamen on the roll fifty more would be sent up to the front to enable me to relieve the force holding Weraroa which, though I regarded it as absolutely useless, local superstition had invested with so much importance in the mind of the Wanganui native and European public. My force, including all the remaining men of No. 6 A. C. and certain fragments of other divisions, with a few men whom I still had on pay of the temporary local forces, was not above 160 in number. The Wanganui friendly natives had long disappeared, and Titokowaru in my front was building a *pah* at the edge of the bush with 700 followers.

The government meanwhile was doing its best to enrol and equip further recruits. But in those days, and under Mr. Stafford's government, loans were not utilised for the defence of the colony, and the sums voted were insufficient for such an emergency as now stared us in the face. Economy therefore was imperative, though with singular courage Mr. Stafford and Colonel Haultain did all that could possibly be done with such means as were obtainable, and strained every nerve to support me. Consequently, though as yet without sufficient force, I felt justified in attempting to hold my ground close to Titokowaru if he permitted me to do so. The detachment of Wanganui militia, all smart lads under Captain Powell who had relieved Sub-Inspector Mc-Donnell at Weraroa, had enabled that officer to rejoin my field force with his detachment of thirty men.

Day by day a stray recruit joined my ranks, and at length, on the 12th, the Defence Minister to my great relief arrived at my head-quarters. He announced the arrival at Wanganui of a new Division No. 7 under Sub-Inspector Brown and their march to join me. He also brought some twenty more Wanganui militia who were all that he could get to relieve Captain Powell's force next day according to promise at Weraroa. Unluckily No. 7 Division did not reach the camp till after dark, and such was the universal terror which Titokowaru's cannibal atrocities had created, that I feared these young soldiers would hardly get through the night without a panic.

This actually occurred. I had lain down fully dressed in expectation of something of this kind, having only recently returned from visiting the sentries, when one of these latter created an alarm by firing his rifle. I knew that this must have been a recruit's folly, and was almost instantly on the ground, among the men who, huddled together behind the parapet, were spreading a senseless panic in the camp. However, by sternly rebuking the officers for not restoring order, and ordering the divisions to fall in at once, and the rolls to be called, we soon got them into some sort of order, and were able to turn in again and finish our night's rest. One recruit, however, disappeared and deserted in the panic.

The Defence Minister was much impressed with this proof of how much remained to be done before our men could be relied on, and when he further heard the Weraroa garrison firing heavily all night, and next day saw how long a flank I must leave open to attack every time I moved with reinforcements or supplies to that point past Titokowaru's position, he resolved that the redoubt was not worth the risk of its retention. Firstly, to have done so meant an immediate deduction of thirty men from the field force as only twenty instead of fifty militia had come up; and, secondly, it was clear that to keep open communication with the redoubt must have involved an abandonment of every other duty of the field force, and compelled it to remain at Nukumaru, whatever Titokowaru might do, in order to fight an almost daily engagement to cover the escort with supplies, along the narrow ridge surrounded by bush which forms the only practical approach.

Colonel Haultain would not thus hamper the only force the government possessed, and was too generous to throw the odium of abandoning the position on me. He therefore gave orders to cause the immediate withdrawal of the garrison, whose time was out, and who must have been relieved at all events at once. All stores that would otherwise fall into the hands of the enemy were ordered to be destroyed. The ammunition was brought off, but the supplies and spirits in the settlers' hut adjoining could not be removed, and the *whare* was consequently burnt. Captain Powell reached the camp without molestation, the whole force being brought up to hold the ground between the enemy and the road. He reported that the redoubt had been fired into during the night, and that the garrison had replied to the shots.

It is probable that the attack was by a reconnoitring party and chiefly intended to discover the strength of the garrison and the position. But the Wanganui lads could not have known how soon the parapet might be swarming with assailants, and their behaviour was admirable. They remained all night under arms, firing at any suspicious object, or replying to any shot directed towards them, with perfect coolness and confidence. Their behaviour showed how much assistance we should have derived from the Wanganui militia, if it had at this critical time turned out, until we were able to obtain recruits.

I do not propose to examine the *pros* and *cons* of the vexed question why at this sole place in New Zealand public danger failed to induce the adult male population to turn out under arms in accordance with the militia law. Auckland, New Plymouth, Napier, Wellington, and even Tauranga and Opotiki, had always complied with the requirements of the law; but from one cause or another it broke down at Wanganui. It was not a new difficulty, it was a resistance to authority of some months date, which in all probability would not have arisen in the beginning if the enemy had then, as now, been almost upon them. With two companies of H. M.'s 18th to protect their town and families, at no place could the requirements of the Militia Act have been more easily or safely carried out. But men had become stiff-necked in their opposition, which the government, in such troublous times, had no power to put down.

Personally, I had but an imperfect knowledge of the condition of things in the district, and, moreover, I had really no command over it, and had only taken upon me to enter it in order to try to keep between the enemy and the settlements. So, I did not interfere, though I urged on the government the absolute necessity of enrolling a special force which might be relied upon at all times to confront the increasing force of Titokowaru, rather than attempt to rely on a law which had at all events in this instance proved inoperative.

Colonel Haultain remained but a short time in my camp, and returned to Wanganui, where the Governor and Premier had arrived. I set myself to work to try to train my recruits a little, and to teach them at least how to use arms which many had never handled before. The inexplicable inaction of the enemy so close to our front lost him his golden opportunity to complete his already unequalled triumphs by stamping out the small force opposed to him. Had he resolutely attacked my lines before the last recruits joined, or even directly after, as they were hardly reliable at first, he should have been able to destroy us. He had three times our force, his men were flushed with success, they were active and well-armed, and even granting that we had shown a stubborn resistance, the issue could not have been doubtful. A nucleus might, and would have fought bravely, but the great bulk of the force might too probably have given way, though so doing might have caused a massacre.

Happily, however, after a few days, Titokowaru's opportunity was lost, and I desired no better than to be attacked by daylight in force. I had little dread of a night attack. Natives, with all their courage, are of little use in the dark, and never willingly move during night. I may except the Uriweras from this, as they are singular in conducting their operations during that portion of the twenty-four hours. But I was pretty confident Titokowaru would not, and the result justified my confidence. I now waited on His Excellency at Wanganui, but nothing was decided, nor indeed could be decided, except to endeavour to obtain reinforcements. The militia clearly would not turn out, or at least so it seemed; and as to the natives, Te Keepa had strongly advised me to have nothing to do with them unless the force raised were picked men, and actually sworn in and enrolled. I therefore returned to my camp, and had the satisfaction of finding the men daily gaining more confidence in themselves, and more expertness with their weapons.

CHAPTER 5

Recalled to the East Coast

I had in my force men who amounted to 350 all told, and recruits to a larger number were daily expected. There were also a few mounted men, but not enough to be used independently in action, though sufficient to meet requirements of postal communication. Unexpectedly I received a despatch from the Defence Minister. By it I was informed that the orders that it contained were imperative, and that they must be implicitly obeyed without remonstrance or delay, as circumstances had rendered them absolutely necessary. I was directed to fall back with all my force behind the Kai-iwi stream, and so dispose them as to hold that line of defence. No orders could have been more unwelcome. I was daily gaining strength both from increasing efficiency and the number of my force. The enemy, who had permitted me to hold my ground when so weak, could not now by attacking me have gained any advantage. The settlers were beginning to regain confidence, and the stock was still on their locations, and if these were not removed with me would be lost when I retired.

But for the imperative expressions of the despatch I would have ridden to Wanganui to assure the Minister that I could hold my ground and, with reinforcements, resume the offensive. But reading between the lines of my orders, I felt sure that some misfortune unknown as yet to me had occurred, and that this retrograde movement was dictated by stern necessity. I therefore immediately and loyally obeyed the instructions, but I decided that these did not amount to requiring such haste as might oblige me to abandon any public or private property in my camp, or prevent my doing my best to remove the settlers' stock.

The news of our retreat was accordingly conveyed to all those settlers whom I could reach, and every cart or waggon was impounded for the settlers' baggage. The sheep and cattle first began to move, collected by the settlers aided by my mounted men, then the carts loaded to the top, and the guns and ammunition followed. Then the troops in the blinding rain fell in, and took the Wanganui road, halting behind each ridge. Lastly, the small cavalry force, insignificant in numbers, and therefore I hoped likely to provoke attack, spread over a large extent of country, as a covering rear-guard of skirmishers. The enemy showed outside his *pah*. But whether the rain or the prospects of a conflict in the open deterred him, I do not know.

This was disappointing. In the open I believed we could fight and win against double our numbers, and would dearly have liked to have made ourselves felt before withdrawing. But it was not to be. The enemy would not follow us, though we moved slowly and halted often in that hope. Nor even did he molest our mounted skirmishers, who endeavoured to provoke and induce him to come on. We could therefore do nothing beyond retreating as we were ordered, except helping as much as possible the poor settlers whose stock was necessarily driven off to save it from the enemy.

It was not a pleasant task. Settler after settler asked me, who was powerless, what he was to do with his stock when he drove it beyond the country to fresh pastures where it could not be grazed, and of course I could give them no assurance either of compensation or even of grazing ground. It was a sad day in my life, a continual recurrence of episodes most grievous to a soldier and a colonist. I needed all my convictions that so high-minded a soldier as Colonel Haultain must have had abundant reason or he would not have given so imperative an order. But my orders were carried out before nightfall, all public and private property in my camp and such stock as could be collected behind the new frontier line.

Thus, from the Waingongoro to the Kai-iwi the rebels had possession of a district recently settled and occupied by our fellow-colonists except where our flag still flew at Patea and Wairoa, which were strong enough to hold their own and protect as much ground as their rifles covered outside. I made the best disposition of the troops as I could in a hurried manner, and then, having accomplished my painful task, rode into Wanganui to ascertain if possible, the reading of the riddle which without some light I could not decipher.

It was speedily afforded me. The district of Poverty Bay near Turanganui, now called Gisborne, had been surprised by Te Kooti in the night and the settlers, including Major Biggs, the R.M., and his young wife and child with many others of both sexes, had been murdered at their homes or in their beds, and a tragedy enacted which on so large a scale was without a parallel in the story of our struggles with the native tribes of New Zealand.

The government, without a force except my own with the smallest pretence of discipline, was doing its best. It had engaged native allies, arming them and paying them for the protection of the settlement, and had given Mr. McLean, their agent at Napier, where he was also Superintendent, the fullest powers to take all steps he might deem necessary for the public safety. Mr. Stafford gave him his *carte blanche*, which was all he could give. He had no men, and had already exhausted every effort to raise even the small force with me. It was evident that till the East Coast was in safety we could not attempt any risk on the West. To advance with half the numerical force of Titokowaru and with untrained men was not, of course, a step any government could have sanctioned.

Mr. McLean was sanguine that with the native allies alone he could recover our prestige and restore tranquillity to Poverty Bay. And while he made the attempt, I was to contract my defence to within the limit of the Kai-iwi stream, and erect blockhouses on which the settlers could retreat if Titokowaru's men made raids towards us. Recruits continued to join me, and the defensive line was clearly defined in front of Woodall's redoubt, and between that point and the sea. The Defence Minister at length explained to me a further dilemma of the government, caused by a despatch from Mr. McLean pressing the sending at least of 200 European troops. These were not as yet enrolled in New Zealand, unless by weakening my force, and yet if Poverty Bay was to be saved no one better than Mr. McLean knew that undisciplined natives would never accomplish it.

Meanwhile, every obstacle had been placed in the way of the government, and the local press had informed the colony that a massacre had occurred through laches of the Stafford Ministry. Mr. McLean was the trusted and confidential agent, but he never once accepted the true responsibility of the disaster, every ounce of which should have been borne by him unless he sheltered himself under that of a subordinate officer, Major Biggs, who no longer lived to tell the world what, if any, orders he had received from the government agent.

I know the facts pretty well, as I knew all the actors in the foregoing, and I limit my accusations of Mr. McLean to absolute and stolid apathetic indifference. I honestly believe he gave no thought to Major Biggs, or Poverty Bay, and that he did not share Mr. Richmond's terrible anxiety any more than he did his political responsibility. I received from Major Biggs, some days after his death, an explanation which I thoroughly believe. He knew Te Kooti was advancing. He knew, he told me, every detail of his force and its numbers, and knew that Poverty Bay was its destination. He said he knew the settlers must be called in, but feeling what it must entail upon them, he had hesitated to expose them to such sacrifices till the last moment; now, however, he must do so, and next day he would.

Alas, poor fellow!—one of the bravest and gentlest men in the colony, he and his wife of a year and their newly-born infant all perished that night, and Mr. McLean used their fate as a means of exciting the public and political opinion against the government, which had treated and trusted him with a magnanimity he hardly deserved or was able to appreciate. Meanwhile, I had laid before government a memorandum offering to go myself with all the men who were really trustworthy, and to leave the district in the interior fully defended. This memorandum the government considered for some days, and they finally adopted my suggestions.

I asked for two or three days, and, at the end of that time, undertook to embark my most reliable European troops, after having placed Wairoa and Patea in a position of safety, and disposed my remaining troops on the Kai-iwi frontier line so as to protect Wanganui. I might mention here that while a few infantry scattered along the river might have deterred the enemy from crossing, and given some feeling of confidence to our settlers, it was impossible to ensure absolute safety to all the scattered homesteads and stock more inland and easily approached through the bush by unperceived foraging parties of the enemy moving early in the morning or at night. One single Maori might probably, if sufficiently well acquainted with the country, have done immense harm with one box of matches and then escaped unseen and unharmed into the recesses of the bush.

It will therefore be understood what value in protecting the district, now the last remaining, I placed upon the two corps of cavalry volunteers which had enrolled themselves. The larger one was composed of young men, chiefly active, energetic young fellows, good riders, and having a considerable knowledge of the whole country. The corps, wearing a gay uniform, and with a great deal of the tone and aspirations of the dragoon, was commanded by Captain Finnimore, and among its members was Mr. John Ballance, subsequently distinguished in another arena. The remaining corps was almost exclusively composed of actual country yeoman settlers, men to whom the saddle was their accustomed resting-place, and who knew every nook and corner of the district. Hardly a farm holding but was represented in their ranks, and they were under the command of Lieutenant John Bryce, an officer who possessed all their confidence, and who for many years almost continuously represented them in Parliament.

Oddly enough, he and Mr. Ballance both distinguished themselves in politics, and held the same portfolios in the Cabinet subsequent to the dark times which I have described, having been opposed in politics, though with a very thin line of difference in the intention of their native policy, albeit, seeking to attain their objects by different methods. It was, to a large extent, upon the devotion and energy of these highly competent mounted corps that I relied for the defence of the settlements in those parts of the district, especially those which were beyond reach of our outposts to our right. Nor was I mistaken in my anticipations, Mr. Bryce's corps, though not so showy as Captain Finnimore's, was, for all the duties of frontier mounted infantry, absolutely perfect, and by continually moving about patrolling and scouting they preserved, in my opinion, the whole of the homesteads to our right flank and right rear from being burnt and plundered by adventurous raiders from Titokowaru's camp.

The two main roads leading north from Wanganui could therefore be protected by the force remaining after I had selected those to go to Poverty Bay. My numbers were increasing daily, and the recruits could be easily trained at the outposts' camp. I knew also that considerable reinforcements might soon be expected from Australia, where a certain number were being enrolled, and I decided that if Patea and Wairoa were sufficiently manned and supplied for a month or more they could hold out well. A little inquiry convinced me that as regarded supplies Patea, which was accessible by sea, was not in danger. Wairoa had been usually provisioned from time to time from Patea, and this might be an embarrassment during my absence.

I therefore resolved to move forward and throw supplies into Wairoa, and acquaint the garrison of the intention to withdraw to the East Coast the fully trained Division No. 1 at Patea, and replace it with younger soldiers, who would be nearly as useful on the defensive. These plans were all made, and the necessary steps were taken next morning, when a foraging party of the enemy came to the Kai-iwi, opposite to Woodall's redoubt, then my headquarters, and set fire to Mr. Moore's house on the other side. It was very provoking, and so meant, no doubt. But it was clearly not an attack in force that was intended, and I was compelled, for fear of losing valuable time, to refrain from advancing my troops, or in any way committing my force to operations at this point.

Next day, November 22nd, I took my first steps towards carrying out the plans approved by the government, by ordering all the available cavalry to communicate with Wairoa, and ascertain exactly the state of that post, and the condition and quantity of its provisions. Captain Newland, of the A. C., commanded; but a volunteer officer of the Patea light horse, with a few men, and Lieutenant John Bryce, with his Kai-iwi cavalry, were with Captain Newland. As the operation has become one to which great public attention has been drawn by a Mr. Rusden, whose libellous attack upon Mr. Bryce has been decided distinctly in favour of the latter by the highest Court of the realm, I might here quote the despatch sent to me by Captain Newland on his return to camp:—

> I must acknowledge the assistance rendered to me by Captain O'Halloran, of the Patea yeomanry cavalry, and Lieutenant Bryce, commanding Kai-iwi and Wanganui cavalry. These gentlemen were prominent in this affair, and set their men a gallant example.

The surprise of Titokowaru's stragglers was complete, though apparently but few were overtaken. The moral effect of the demonstration, as showing that we were not unprepared to move, was valuable, and the reports from Wairoa were highly satisfactory. Captain Hawes and his garrison, who were all *bona fide* country settlers, were in good heart, and resolved to hold their post, which was strongly fortified, commanded a considerable space of open ground, and was well supplied with ammunition, biscuits, and groceries. The meat supplies were deficient, and if these were increased Captain Hawes, who was informed of our intentions, felt he could hold his own.

On the 29th, therefore, I ordered Colonel Gorton at Wanganui to direct seventy-two recruits to escort drays for Wairoa with sheep and supplies to the mouth of the Kai-iwi River, and Colonel Noake to call out 100 militia to proceed to Stewart's redoubt, and to cover the erection of a blockhouse while he was to send on Captain Finnimore's cavalry, so as to reach Kai-iwi mouth before nightfall. I resigned myself to do without Lieutenant Bryce's corps, because that officer had reported that he had reason to believe the enemy's foragers would attempt to plunder and destroy some of the homesteads to my right, and I had therefore given him open orders the previous day to patrol and reconnoitre in that direction.

On the 30th I moved off with the bulk of my force, crossing the country to the sea-coast road, and meeting the drays and column some small distance short of Nukumaru.

I felt sure the enemy's foragers on my right would speedily retire when they heard of my advance, and was confident that Mr. Bryce's corps, if they discovered them, would hasten their retreat and inflict some punishment upon them. All this occurred, and Lieutenant Bryce was enabled to protect, at all events, one homestead (Dr. Mussen's) from destruction; and if another (late Mr. Hewitt's) was burned it was the sole one injured, and burned apparently in revenge by the retreating foragers, who had probably suffered losses from Mr. Bryce's cavalry.

On December 2nd I embarked on board the steamers *Sturt* and *Ladybird* 212 men of the armed constabulary, with whom I sailed for Poverty Bay. No better proof could be given of the progress of discipline in the force than the circumstance that not a single man was absent, although some of them had marched the day before in a blinding dust-storm from Patea. I left behind me 230 of the armed constabulary, besides some sixty more recruits who had taken the place of No. 1 Division, at Patea; and in all 392 men, more or less disciplined, together with some country militia on pay and protecting the blockhouses. There were, it is true, 700 militia of the first and second class besides, including those who lived immediately beyond the river; so that, in all, there were 1200 men of all ranks to defend the town, besides two companies of Her Majesty's 18th Regiment, who were restricted by their orders from taking part in offensive operations.

I accordingly arrived on December 4th at Poverty Bay, where I found the Hon. Mr. J. C. Richmond, who informed me that I should have no trouble with the natives as Mr. McLean had written to them urging them to preserve discipline and obey my orders. Long afterwards Mr. Richmond stated in Parliament what the text of these letters was. He said (on June 18th, 1869):—

When I went to Napier and told my hon. friend (Mr. McLean) that Colonel Whitmore was coming he repeated his protests that the arrival of Colonel Whitmore would be the signal for the dispersion of the native troops. I said it was too late to prevent his coming... I also told the hon. member the country re-

quired that he should use his efforts to prevent that dispersion...
My hon. friend did not promptly respond to that duty, but, after
a little hesitation, gave me letters to the chiefs urging them not
to return upon Colonel Whitmore's arrival. The hon. member
had the candour to give them to me open, and I thought it no
breach of confidence, under the circumstances, to read them. I
mention it here to show the spirit in which my hon. friend was
carrying out the wishes of the government. I will read one of
his letters:—

> To Ropata and Hotene Te Ngatiporo. Friends, saluta-
> tions! Listen you two. It is not of my doing that Colonel
> Whitmore is going thither to do the work which has
> been so nearly finished by you. But now he has got there,
> you must unite in attacking the *Hau-Haus*. . . .
> Mr. Richmond will be there to give directions in case of
> any troubles arising out of Colonel Whitmore's manage-
> ment.
>
> Your friend, McLean.

This quotation is quite sufficient to show the spirit in which the
government agent seconded the efforts of the government.

NGATA PAH—SITUATED ON THE CREST OF THE HILL.

CHAPTER 6

The Fall of Ngatapa

After the massacre Te Kooti remained in the vicinity foraging, plundering, and recruiting from the local friendlies, and removing whatever booty he could carry towards a position he had selected called Ngatapa, some days' march to his rear. By this time the agent of the government, Mr. McLean, to whom *carte blanche* had been given by Mr. Stafford, had assembled a horde of friendly Maoris from the coast to the north and south. This multitude, to which very few Europeans were attached, slowly pushed Te Kooti back to the vicinity of Ngatapa.

While this movement was going on Te Kooti, mustering a few followers, deliberately went round the flank of the friendlies and marching rapidly, succeeded in surprising an escort of ammunition close to Patutahi, close to Gisborne, carrying off a large supply. With this he got back safely to his force, where he was received with acclamations, not only because his foray had been successful, but because it seemed the fulfilment of the prophecy he had made before he marched that he would come back laden with cartridges.

Mr. McLean was too well acquainted with the natives not to be aware that a force of nothing but friendlies would prove costly, useless, and unmanageable for prolonged operations, and he therefore now appealed to the government to despatch as soon as possible an adequate European contingent. I was accordingly despatched by steamer to Poverty Bay; No. 8 Division, recruited among the Arawas and commanded by Captain Grundy, joined me there, together with a few recruits from Canterbury, raising the force to about 300 men. With the force under my command I reached Poverty Bay, and landed on December 4th.

At Wanganui the greatest consternation prevailed, notwithstanding the fact that a regular though not as yet very highly trained force of 400 men remained in position on the Kai-iwi between the enemy and the town, which, in addition to its own excellent volunteer cavalry and town and suburban militia, was further protected by two companies of H. M. 2—18th. Regiment. The local militia and volunteers were or should have been 1500 in number, and Colonel McDonnell was authorized, at his own suggestion, to raise an auxiliary force of friendly Maoris.

Why, therefore, the West Coast should have so strongly objected to afford so small a contingent to aid the settlers of Poverty Bay and the East Coast, from which in its own extremity the only existing force had been brought round to help them after the Ngutu-o-te-manu, was a question difficult to solve. But the government wisely refused to be influenced by this clamour, and met the emergency in the only possible manner by remaining on the defensive upon the West Coast, training recruits as they arrived there in the meanwhile, and turning all its efforts to the crushing of Te Kooti if possible before he could do any further harm.

When I landed at Poverty Bay the first report handed to me led me to believe that this object had in a great measure been accomplished. Popular feeling was at the time much excited against the government, upon whom the blame of the massacre was most unfairly thrown. The agent on the coast, Mr. McLean, who was of course the actually responsible person, escaping the odium, through the circumstances of his position, Mr. McLean being bitterly opposed to the government. As I was well known to serve the government with the devotion a military officer is bound in honour to show, there was perhaps no mode of showing hostility, opposition or ill-will that was omitted on the part of very many of those surrounding me when I landed. All were exultant at the Maori success (as it was reported to be), and evinced no jealousy whatever at the accomplishment of the service of native auxiliaries alone.

I was assured that the settlement was perfectly secure, and emphatically told that to the natives and not to the government the thanks of the settlement were due. But a very few hours sufficed to show that all this congratulation had been premature, and that the locality was by no means as yet in safety. In point of fact a success had been gained at an irregular engagement at Makaretu, where the enemy had suffered a loss variously stated at from fifteen to sixty men. Subsequently, from the accounts of prisoners, the true number was ascertained to be four-

MAJOR KEEPA RANGIHIWINUI, N.Z.C.

SERGEANT C. MALING, N.Z.C.

MAJOR ROPATA, N.Z.C.

teen. From Makaretu, the scene of the engagement, Te Kooti retreated to Ngatapa, a position at that time not fully fortified, and Ropata, the gallant chief of the Ngatiporos, with seventy of his own *hapu*, followed him up, and gallantly endeavoured to force an entrance.

But the Napier natives and the rest of his own tribe left their valiant leader unsupported, and after holding his own till after nightfall, when he found entrance impossible, Ropata fell back, being without food or ammunition. The inflated accounts of this engagement, however, imposed a great deal upon Mr. Richmond, the Native Minister, and myself. We concluded that there must have been more success than a mere repulse of Te Kooti, as the native force had been as four to one in the open field; and when Mr. Gascoigne, who had been sent to reconnoitre, returned and said that Te Kooti had burned his camp and retreated, we felt satisfied at first that the settlement was free of the outlaw for a time.

Therefore, when Ropata asked to return to his home and change his men, and the Napier natives pressed for leave to return to their home, I offered no great resistance. Ropata promised to return in a week, and I felt sure he at least would keep his word, for his settlement was far away to the north and beyond European political intrigue, and by a week's time we should know if we had or had not been deceived with respect to Te Kooti's retreat.

The Napier natives left first, but Ropata and his men had not yet embarked when some of Te Kooti's prisoners escaped, bringing me intelligence that the enemy were still at Ngatapa and meant to come down once more on Turanganui. This intelligence decided me to land No. 6 Division, already embarked to return to the West Coast, and to move up towards Patutahi. Ropata brought back his force. But the day (13th) wore on and no sign of the enemy was discovered till 3 p.m., when I received a report that he had made a raid upon Te Arai, where Ihaka Whanga with his Mahia natives, sent by me to patrol that locality, had fired upon him and driven him back.

This intelligence decided me to push on, but unfortunately it came too late. The cavalry (sixteen) had been sent on the way to Ngatapa early in the morning, but had discovered no trace of Te Kooti; but at 4 p.m. his force was descried retreating inland towards Ngatapa, about four miles from the entrance of the gorge. Our men had but three miles to march to anticipate him at the gorge, but such was the speed with which Te Kooti conducted his march that our men were distanced in the race and could only follow and fire upon him as he retired. Our cavalry, however, returning from their reconnaissance, met Te Kooti in the valley, but failing to delay or attack him, and preferring to seek safety in flight, Captain Newland was of no assistance to the column in pursuit.

Ropata now left the Bay to collect a reliable force of 300 men, and I prepared to beat up Te Kooti's quarters at Ngatapa as soon as I could prepare a commissariat supply for the operations it was now evident that we must carry out. Pack animals and drivers had to be collected both to feed the force and to bring up ammunition and stores. Some days were occupied in preparation, but we ultimately moved forward and reached the extreme point to which sumpter animals could go on December 27th. This spot I fortified and called Fort Richmond, in honour of the Native Minister whose presence and assistance were of the utmost importance and value to me. From this point the fortifications of Ngatapa were plainly visible. It was what in civilized warfare would be called a hill fort with triple line of enormously strong parapet defences unnecessarily thick, indeed proof against ordinary field artillery, protecting the summit of a conical hill rising some 800 feet from the bottom of a ravine which intervened between it and Fort Richmond.

The descent and ascent of this ravine was too steep for horses, and it was evident that I must rely entirely upon packing all requisites, even ammunition, on the men's backs. The Ngatiporos returned to the day, but their march to Ngatapa was delayed by the illness of their chief Ropata. Mr. Richmond, unfortunately, had not supplied them with ammunition on landing, being provoked at their returning without the supply they had taken to their homes. The great difficulty of carriage made this very embarrassing, for I had to exhaust the reserve I had brought up with so much difficulty in issuing the usual amount per man. Directly Ropata joined me I moved on, halting for the night 700 yards from the fort, and giving orders for the investment or partial investment at dawn next day. My information had been so good that this operation was carried out with the most perfect success, notwithstanding the rugged nature of the ground and denseness of the forest.

Before night my headquarters were about 300 yards from the front line of defence, the defenders were cut off from water, and I had concentrated all round the line of investment. I had a Cohorn mortar and some shells with me, and these I used with advantage during what may be called the siege. Unfortunately, our force was insufficient for a complete investment, and I had to neglect some fifty or sixty yards of

SECTIONS OF
NGATAPA PA
POVERTY BAY

Scale in feet

what seemed a sheer precipice. I had relied upon the Napier natives to complete the investing force, but Mr. McLean had despatched the Napier native force to Puketapu from which Te Kooti had marched two months before, which was found, as might have been expected, unoccupied. Thus, the auxiliaries who would have been of infinite value at Ngatapa were many miles away when required.

The enemy being without water, it was hoped the operations would not occupy much time, for the supply of some 700 men under such difficulties was exhausting to the men employed in packing food; but as the night closed in and the parapet of a parallel had been thrown up, it began to rain and rained for three days and nights consecutively. My native force kept up its spirits by continuous firing all day and night, consuming so much ammunition as to threaten serious inconvenience. Mr. Richmond, however, charged himself with bringing up a supply and, together with Captain Twogood, left in the night with that object.

At the township no aid could be got, but these gentlemen almost alone did eventually succeed in procuring and bringing up the requisite ammunition in a cart which they drove themselves. Through the rain the Europeans pushed forward their approaches, with great difficulty and some loss. The rebel natives, unable to get rest owing to the intermittent fire of the Cohorn at irregular periods, and beginning to find their position desperate, made several determined, but except on one occasion, ineffectual attempts to break through the line especially towards the rear where Major Fraser commanded.

I had almost persuaded myself from this that the precipice was regarded as hopeless. January 4th dawned bright and fine. The trenches had been brought to within seventy yards, when at 2 p.m., Ropata agreed to make an attempt to carry the outer parapet, which proved to be almost unflanked. This service was excellently carried out. The natives (Ngatiporos and Arawa A. C.) crept under the crest of the hill through the bush till close to the end of the outer parapet, nearest to the precipice, and then with a cheer and a rush made good a lodgement under its shelter. The Poverty Bay volunteers, who had on this occasion offered their services to atone perhaps for their want of support on a former one, followed the natives in support, and part of the European A. C. joined them with spades to secure the position and make further approaches against the inner works.

I had intended to break through the parapet and seize the two next lines of defence by a dash, as they were wholly unflanked, when

PLAN OF

NGATAPA PA

POVERTY BAY
taken by
COL. WHITMORE *with the* COLONIAL FORCE
from the
HAU HAU *under* TE KOOTI

I met with an unexpected obstacle. My 300 Europeans were of necessity distributed all round the position, or employed carrying stores and ammunition. Without their presence I could not have relied on a vigilant watch being kept on the enemy all round, while the painful and laborious duty of "humping" loads up the slippery hill, the natives absolutely refused to share. Therefore, I was compelled to require at least an equal assaulting party from the Ngatiporo; but they, though willing, even eager for the undertaking, still would not move without taking forty rounds of ammunition per man. Unluckily I could not give that supply to them, and by 5 p.m., when I was in a position to do so, the excitement had evaporated, and I was obliged to postpone the assault till dawn.

During the night progress was made to secure the second entrenchments, which were seized before midnight, while upon the left the Maoris under Wickliffe secured the outer parapet in front of them. Everything promised well for the morning, when, as day broke, a woman calling from inside acquainted us that the enemy had just escaped by the precipice. It was not long before we verified her information, and within a quarter of an hour the pursuit was begun. Ropata undertook this, stipulating that no Europeans should be employed as his men were accustomed to bush work, amply numerous, and as they could go almost naked might not be distinguished from the enemy by the Europeans. Te Kooti had perhaps an hour's start, but was encumbered with wounded, women and baggage, so that in a very short time his rear was overtaken. Throughout the day the pursuit was carried on towards the Uriwera Mountains, and more than 120 were killed, among whom was the only chief of birth, Nikora of the Ngatihineuru, one of the survivors of the fatal day to that tribe at Omaranui, near Napier, in 1866.

It is not my present object to go into the details of these events. A short sketch of the leading features, already given, being all that is necessary to understand the importance of the Uriwera Mountains as a refuge to the natives, and the danger that that comparatively safe place of retreat constituted to the surrounding settlements.

Te Kooti again wounded at Ngatapa was hurried off by his Uriwera allies and safely gained the protection of the mountains. More than half his force slain and driven out of his chosen fortification, it seemed that he must have lost his prestige and become discredited with his followers. But this man proved to possess an influence over, and to be able to implant, a superstitious fanaticism in the minds of all the tribes with which he came in contact, as singular as unaccountable, and although the heavy losses at Ngatapa served as a lesson and deterred further attempts upon Poverty Bay, Te Kooti was soon again at the head of a formidable band and able to repeat his bloodthirsty razzias upon the coast settlements of the Bay of Plenty, from the mountains.

My force being now no longer needed at Poverty Bay so much as at Wanganui, I withdrew the bulk of the men to the West Coast, arriving myself there on January 16th. Here I found a large congregation of the purest recruits and matters in other respects much as I left them. Colonel Lyon, who had taken command, had beaten up Titokowaru's quarters, and the local cavalry under Finnimore and Bryce had also reconnoitred and patrolled the country beyond the Kai-iwi as far as Gentle Annie, on the other side of Patea. Except in a very languid way Titokowaru had not asserted himself or taken advantage of his opportunities. Some few small expeditions by inconsiderable war parties had occurred, but practically he had simply held his ground at Taurangahika since I fell back to Kai-iwi, near Nukumaru, plundering and devastating the district.

All this was now to change. The troops were raw, the appliances of war defective, but the force was numerically strong, and the country was groaning under the reverses we had suffered and the stagnation and misery which the loss of the district had occasioned.

WEST COAST CAMPAIGN

Scale of English Miles

10   0   10   20   30

CHAPTER 7

Resumption of Hostilities on the West Coast

Ngatapa fell on January 5th, 1869. No time was wasted in retiring the troops and returning to the West Coast. My force, reinforced by No. 8 (Arawa) Division of selected enrolled Maoris, was at once sent on by government steamers to Wanganui. I, following in the ordinary passenger steamer, arrived on the 18th, when I received reports from Colonel Lyon and Lieut.-Colonel McDonnell of expeditions each had made to the front. Colonel Lyon had fired some twelve rounds into the *pah* at Taurangahika, and proceeded to Patea, where he found the garrison in good heart. From thence he moved up to Ketemarae and Taiporohenui, where he burnt the village, and returning by Mokoia and Manutahi passed through Patea on his return. In this expedition some horses and cattle were captured, but being claimed by Patea settlers were handed over to them.

Returning from Patea, Colonel Lyon was fired upon by the enemy, but as his object was confined to a reconnaissance he did not delay or bring about an engagement. Lieut.-Colonel McDonnell, with a force principally of mounted natives, had pushed on to Waihi and revisited Ngutu-o-te-manu. Both officers reported that in the district beyond the Patea River there were no apparent signs of the enemy, and that therefore in all probability his whole force was concentrated near Nukumaru.

On the 20th I moved forward to the ford of the Kai-iwi on the inland road. My force was now considerable. No. 4 Division A. C. had joined me from the Waikato. I had, when all should arrive, the Ngatapa force except the garrison of sixty men left at what is now Gisborne, and I had a number of recruits from Australia, who were being trained in camp. Kemp, with a corps of selected natives sworn in and dressed in uniform, had joined, and the force, if efficient, was therefore ample to engage the enemy. But much required to be done before the newly joined troops could be regarded as reliable. They had been, up to this, accustomed to sleep in a single large redoubt, and were hardly prepared to camp without artificial protection. It was obviously my first duty to make my men efficient, and I decided to begin by making them learn to camp by divisions, permitting them to throw up a parapet round their tents.

On the 21st I pushed on Colonel Lyon beyond the bush in front of Woodall's redoubt, where they entrenched themselves. I then began to repair the road and bridge. On the 22nd I further reinforced Colonel Lyon by No. 6 Division A. C. and the native force. On the 23rd all available men were employed on the road, and a party of the enemy advancing in our direction, apparently to forage, was met by Lieutenant Bryce and his cavalry, who, however, by my orders, withdrew to allow the infantry (A. C.) under Captain G. McDonnell to engage them, but they declined to stand, and retreated too precipitately to be intercepted even by a second party under Colonel Lyon, which hurried up by a shorter path.

The Arawa division (No. 8 A. C.) had meanwhile come up, and Captain Finnimore's cavalry, but we could not get an opportunity to use our force. That night the advance consisted of the volunteer cavalry, Kemp's natives, with Nos. 1, 4, and 7 and 8 A. C. We now abandoned Westmere, and the advance movement began. The next day, 24th, being Sunday, we halted in our positions. On the 25th we completed the Kai-iwi bridge, and my whole force was moved beyond the stream.

At daylight next morning my small corps of guides, under Sergeant Maling, pushing on in advance, discovered the enemy and was fired upon. The guides behaved with great gallantry, and compelled the enemy to disclose an ambuscade on the road through the bush which he had evidently prepared for my march; but as they were few in number they were compelled to retire with the loss of one of their men who, being wounded in the leg, was overtaken and tomahawked. I heard the firing while I was moving my headquarters to join the advance, and, hurrying up, pushed on Colonel Lyon with his force and the Arawas, supported by No. 1 Division, by the bush road.

I followed myself, taking Nos. 1 and 8 Divisions, just in time to save the Okehu bridge, which the enemy had set on fire, from being burnt. Kemp, who had preceded me by a different route, now reported the enemy in full retreat, and further pursuit ceased. Final arrangements were now completed for a definite forward movement. Fifty-five recruits were sent back by Wanganui to replace No. 4 A. C. in Waikato, our last Poverty Bay detachment rejoined with Lieut.-Colonel St. John, and all our baggage and carts were brought across the Kai-iwi by the new line of communications.

I moved for the next few days in a very leisurely manner by the inland road on purpose to familiarize my men with camp life. Many in all the divisions were strange to the country, unused to arms, and to some extent influenced by the silly camp gossip of the enemy's atrocities to the wounded and mutilation or worse of the dead. Every hour gained was important. The men were learning not only how to bear themselves before the enemy, but, finding nothing very tremendous to undergo in the way of fatigue, or any danger which they could not easily face, were in a fair way to become soldiers. But I knew that all rested on a very fragile foundation, and while I crept on a few miles a day I carefully avoided leaving any opening for Titokowaru to take my raw troops at a disadvantage.

By the 1st I had reached, or nearly reached, Nukumaru, and was ready to assail Titokowaru's camp. My information was not perfect as to his fortifications, and I was compelled to avoid exposing my force to the smallest risk. Consequently, next day, when we moved forward, I pushed on the cavalry in advance and brought up the infantry under cover of the bush. The *pah* proved to be a most elaborate structure, well flanked, provided with a sort of *machieouli* protection at the entrance and completely hidden from us by the bush. I went myself to reconnoitre the position from a spot not far distant from the jungle; then closed in upon two sides with my infantry.

To prevent casualties, I entrenched the men in their positions, which towards evening were only about seventy yards from the work. Unluckily, the Armstrong guns came up just before dark, and without orders opened fire. I had not intended this, as I wished to reserve all my means of offence till next morning. Meanwhile I got my Cohorn mortars up to the infantry positions with orders to throw shells into the *pah* at daybreak, when I meant to complete the investment.

Our casualties were next to nothing. There had been some firing, but our men were not exposed. The volunteer cavalry had searched the whole of the open or lightly timbered country round the *pah*, without loss, and apparently the enemy had no intention of fighting

94

outside his fortifications. The troops remained in their positions, taking post myself with the guns. The night passed without any occurrence of importance, and just as day was breaking, I began to move my men round the two unattached sides of the *pah*. The Cohorns fired to get the range, and our men moved on. The Armstrong guns opened, too, and in a few minutes, we should have surrounded the enemy. Just now, however, a few daring spirits forestalled the movement, and pushing forward to the *pah*, discovered that it was deserted. Directly this was reported to me I pushed on the cavalry to Weraroa, where it engaged the enemy, and on to Wairoa, beyond the Waitotara, and detaching two columns, one by the direct road to the Karaka flat, and one beyond that and Weraroa, made every effort to overtake the enemy.

I was not sorry that Taurangahika had thus fallen without resistance. My object was to regain possession of the district, and if I could do this without loss, and without putting too heavy a strain on my raw troops, they would be encouraged, while an equal advantage would accrue to the country. I was resolved to push Titokowaru beyond the Waitotara, and consequently the pursuit was pushed on with great rapidity. Major Kemp, and Captain Porter of No. 8 A. C., moving in advance with his picked corps, before long overtook the rear-guard, and engaged it at once. Colonel Lyon, with some 200 men on the Karaka flat, also became engaged some distance to his right, and I from the Weraroa got a column ready to act if required as a support.

Meanwhile I sent Mr. Bryce to Wairoa to communicate with the garrison and report, after searching the neighbourhood, whether there were any signs of the enemy in that direction. Titokowaru, however, continued his retreat inland from Karaka, only leaving a rear-guard under the brow of the hill to delay our advance, while he crossed the Waitotara with all his force, women and baggage, at Papatupu.

Kemp, having lost one man, and his small force having become dispersed in the bush, withdrew towards Weraroa, after extricating the leading men from an ambuscade they had fallen into. Lyon's men, in skirmishing order, wavered, and after three or four had been wounded, first hesitated and halted, and then retreated. Colonel Lyon, as brave an officer as any who ever served Her Majesty, scorned to retire, and remained with his wounded, walking erect from one to the other, a target for the enemy's rear-guard. I lost no time in bringing up supports and withdrawing the wounded, but the day was waning, the men had had no food, the enemy's rear-guard had disappeared, and nothing more could be undertaken that day. I therefore withdrew the troops for the night to Weraroa, where after inquiry I dismissed several of the men who had misbehaved with Lieut.-Colonel Lyon.

Next morning, as soon as it was day, I again moved across the valley to Karaka flat, and made the divisions which had misbehaved move in front. I followed with No. 1, and told the leading divisions I would fire into them if they hesitated again. They did not put me to the test, but moved steadily on, crossing the Karaka smartly, and then descending to the bed of the river at Papatupu, where Titokowaru had crossed. Here the closest search could not discover the direction of the retreat, but it was clear that the enemy had abandoned the Waitotara district. We found the mutilated corpse of Hori, Kemp's missing man, and buried it. His heart had been cut out by the enemy, which produced an extraordinary effect on his comrades. Until I could find out whether the enemy had really retreated, we returned ourselves to our several positions on the Karaka, Weraroa, and Nukumaru after removing all the stock we could find. We were not likely to gain any information of the enemy except by search or guess work.

At first, I decided that the probabilities were that Titokowaru had made off to the north, with the intention of regaining his own district. Before me to the right front, front, and right rear, was an endless expanse of jungle and forest stretched as far as the eye could reach, all unoccupied country, from which no information could be hoped for. Such indications as smoke rising in the bush were watched for in every direction. Two settlers engaged in collecting horses to my right front did, however, fall in with the enemy, and only by dint of great presence of mind and resolute courage escaped to make their report. One was a Mr. Williams; I regret I did not ascertain the name of the other.

On the 5th I had crossed from Weraroa to Wairoa and seen Captain Hawes, the energetic and gallant commander of the post, who informed me that though he had kept up continual patrols of reconnaissance, he had found no trace of the enemy in the direction of Patea or the open country from the bush to the sea. The Okotuku bush track he had not been able to examine, with so small a force, but every other known track had been carefully reconnoitred.

The volunteer cavalry had patrolled the whole country under Lieutenant Bryce with similar results, and I therefore marched with a sufficient force next day to Moturoa and Okotuku to examine the only remaining exit from the Waitotara in the direction of Patea. We found the *pah* at Moturoa as it had been left by the enemy a day or two after my repulse. It was larger and stronger than it had been thought, and covered a space of more than half an acre. It was completely enclosed and, from the ditch dug under the inner palisades, the defenders had fired upon our men in perfect security. It was larger even than Taurengahika, and as it must have been constructed in so short a time, and consisted of two rows of young trees of twelve feet high at least out of the ground, the numbers employed may be imagined, though probably some were women. The outline of the *pah* was irregular, but the angles fairly flanked the work.

We had here the melancholy satisfaction of collecting the remains of our poor comrades who had fallen, and some of whom had been partly eaten by Titokowaru's followers. All that could be found of their remains was too much burned to be recognisable. We carefully and reverently gathered all that could be collected, and removed them to Wairoa cemetery, where at least they received Christian burial. Pushing on from Moturoa up the hill, we examined Okotuku, and I was satisfied that no natives had visited the place for some months. I destroyed the Moturoa as I had the Taurangahika *pah*, burned the huts at Okotuku and the stores of potatoes collected there, and then, concluding that I had overrun the trail of the enemy's retreat, decided that I must, as hunting men say, "hark back."

It was the principle of my operations to push the enemy steadily before me and leave no force which could endanger the settled districts behind. I had abandoned the old system of defending scattered settlements by means of central posts, and I had decided to maintain only my line of communication by the sea coast, while the field force operated on the so-called "inland" road close to the bush, as it was evident that the enemy would no longer, as in former times, come out into the open to fight.

If we were to convince the rebels that their resistance was hopeless, we must be prepared to show them that even in their own formidable bush, and against even the ambuscades and surprises of their traditional warfare, we were able not only to hold our own, but to defeat them. The inland road from the Kai-iwi was not constructed beyond Weraroa, and was indeed only a mere track for the greater part of the way. I had bridged the Kai-iwi and saved the Okehu bridge, and there was no obstacle to my march with my supply wagons and guns up to the Weraroa, which overhung the largest of the coast rivers, the Waitotara. A very little examination showed me I must make a barrel-pier pontoon or bridge, at a still spot below the Weraroa, and construct a road from the redoubt to the stream, or else the inland line could not be utilized further north. This accordingly was my first step on recrossing from Wairoa, and I sent to collect the necessary material for the bridge or pontoon.

I now distributed my troops, leaving a strong force on the brow of the Karaka plateau overlooking the bend of the river at Papatupu, and placed Lieut.-Colonel McDonnell, who had joined me, in command. I took the headquarters and the bulk of the impedimenta, guns, wagons, &c., with a portion of the force to Nukumaru which, being on the usual line of communication, was easily supplied. Seeing that the operations would be mainly now in the bush, I released Major Finnimore's troop of volunteer cavalry, with thanks for their valuable services, and they returned to their homes. Lieutenant Bryce's troop, being composed of country settlers, I left to guard the district and to patrol the country, Colonel Lyon being placed at Kai-iwi in command with a portion of the force.

Meanwhile, I had relaxed no effort to find the direction of Titokowaru retreat, Lieut.-Colonel McDonnell and Major Kemp having been energetic in making reconnaissances to the right with that object. These operations I will presently describe more in detail. On February 6th, I established my headquarters at Nukumaru, where I was visited by the commodore of the station who, with General Chute, had come to assist in the capture of Taurengahika, if the operation had, as anticipated, proved a difficult one.

Finding, however, that the enemy had been dislodged, and that further operations must necessarily be of a character in which artillery or rocket fire could be of little service, and there could be no estimate formed of their duration, the commodore was unable to see any way in which he could usefully co-operate. Nevertheless, he was much disappointed, as indeed I was myself, as the intention was generous and in entire keeping with the high spirit which invariably distinguishes the noble service to which he belonged.

Dr. Featherston, weak and suffering in health, but with that fiery spirit and iron nerve he had so often shown in the service of the country, now, though politically opposed to the government, tendered me his assistance, than which none could be more influential with the native tribes, and offered to accompany me through the campaign to be at hand if I should require it to be exerted. The Hon. Dr. Grace, M.L.C., then in a leading practice at Wellington, knowing that New Zealand had sent her soldiers to fight her battles with next to no medical assistance, voluntarily left his practice and came to my camp while Taurengahika was being attacked, to lend his aid in the treatment of the wounded of our force. I especially note these two gentlemen because it impressed itself in my memory that, after all, there was at all events among the more high-minded and educated of our fellow-colonists still to be found that true spirit of nationality which sinks all minor questions, and flinches from no personal sacrifice when the public safety is endangered. And they were not the only instances of that encouragement and sympathy which none can appreciate so well as a soldier in the field.

From all parts of New Zealand, I received from leading men letters from some, offers of personal assistance from others, recognising my difficulties, and wishing me well. There were, I am ashamed to say, among the leaders of the opposition in Parliament notable exceptions and even instances of intriguing with my subordinate officers, sometimes brought to my knowledge by their showing me themselves the letters, and refusing to be drawn into a correspondence evidently intended to hamper me, and to be paid for by promotion when Mr. Stafford's government succumbed.

Dr. Grace told me how precarious Dr. Featherston's health had become, and that while he would certainly not be deterred from carrying out his offer by anything short of my own declining it, his doing so would in all probability prove dangerous to his life. I need not say that, under these circumstances, I wrote to the doctor to prevent his coming, but I acknowledged in the most grateful terms the generosity and unselfishness of his offer, and the very great value I attached to his influence. Often since I had wished he had been well enough to have come, for he was an unflinching lover of the truth, so shamelessly perverted by his own party in the subsequent debates of Parliament, and without regard to persons would have given his testimony truthfully, whatever the result.

I endeavoured to counteract the falsehoods of the press by directing that every correspondent who came to the field should be given rations, tentage, and forage, and furnished on application to the brigade major with any details he could safely publish. I was aware that several came to my camp, though only in one or two instances did I know them by appearance. I believe two or more were recalled and lost their employment because all their accounts contradicted what was wished to be confirmed, and had been so freely asserted, as to the operations in progress. In fact, the truth was not wanted, and as in spite of these punishments by way of examples, *pour encourager les autres,* it soon became evident that as regular correspondents could not be induced even by this means so far to falsify facts to oblige their employers, they were all before long withdrawn.

The position at Waitotara was unsatisfactory in the extreme. We watched the river from above the Karaka to the sea, and had reason to believe that the enemy had not attempted to return. We could only conclude that he was still encamped in the gorge of the Momahaki stream, an affluent of the Waitotara, which falls into it at the Papatupu bend from the ranges to the north and eastward of that river. All that area being covered with dense forest, extreme vigilance to prevent any sudden movement by the enemy was required. On February 16th I sent out a patrol of 180 men, chiefly volunteers, to endeavour to intercept any straggling parties from the enemy's camp towards Okotuku or Patea. On the 17th, Colonel McDonnell crossed the Waitotara and reconnoitred in an easterly direction. On the 18th, Kemp returned, having indeed found traces of straggling parties digging potatoes at Putahi, but without discovering anything reliable about the main body.

On the same day a party of one sergeant and nine men from Colonel McDonnell's camp at Karaka crossed the Waitotara to forage for peaches in the groves of the opposite valley. They had scarcely reached the peach grove before they were fired upon from an ambuscade, and though they had their arms with them, were overpowered and tomahawked while attempting to make good their retreat to their canoe, only three escaping. The sergeant's body was mutilated and a portion of it carried away presumably to furnish a cannibal feast. Lieut. -Col. McDonnell turned out his division on hearing the firing, and hurried down to the spot where the men had crossed, but except to exchange a few volleys with the enemy's ambuscade party, estimated at seventy to a hundred natives, it was impossible to do anything.

On the 19th, having been rejoined by Major Swindley's column, which had been scouting in the direction of Okotuku, I sent No. 8, the Arawa Division, and Major Kemp's natives across the Waitotara near the peach grove, whence the enemy, who still seemed to be about, fired a volley or two and made off. Lieut.-Colonel McDonnell's Division moved across in support. I brought my headquarters to Weraroa, and pressed on the work of roadmaking to the place where the punt was being constructed and to the pack road towards Papatupu required to ration the men. The Arawa Division during their day's skirmish had behaved well, and pressed on eagerly to close with the enemy, admirably supported by Lieut.-Col. McDonnell's men who were anxious to avenge their comrades. The rebel party, however, would not stand, and made off into the densest of the hush as quickly as possible.

I now resolved to hurry matters a little, and to endeavour to find the enemy in the bush, or failing this, to construct a track easy for our men to march by more quickly than they could move by the narrow, crooked footpaths. I had, too, to train my men to be steady in the bush, for they seemed lamentably alarmed at its imaginary dangers. I therefore distributed the force along a line leading more or less in the direction of Okotuku, and cleared a way half a chain wide of brushwood and "supplejacks." I made the men sleep in small detachments along this line where they worked, and although the first night there was a great deal of wholly unnecessary firing, still they gradually got habituated to the bush, and ceased to feel the terror which it once inspired. Practically, I did not attach much importance to the road, but a great deal to rendering the men reliable in the bush, where I foresaw, we should henceforward have to meet the enemy.

This work occupied the troops to the end of February, and as it was evidently not Titokowaru's intention to retreat at once, and he might prolong his stay in the ranges for some time, I took the opportunity of visiting Wellington to confer with the government and press for a native Ngatiporo contingent to follow the enemy in the bush.

Meanwhile I had made every preparation to move on, with the utmost rapidity, directly Titokowaru was known not to have taken up any position in or near the settled country either in front or rear of my own. Unfortunately, a great flood in the Waitotara occurred at the end of February, necessitating the withdrawal of my detachments beyond it, and carrying away my barrel-punt. Much of the country was inundated both in the Momahaki valley and in that of the Waitotara. The rivers of the West Coast have so much fall and, though short, have such deep beds owing to the force of the current that they fill rapidly and overflow often in a few hours. The removal of the road-cutting detachments was therefore a necessity and achieved only just in time, as we found afterwards that the trees in the valley where the men had been working were marked with mud and debris up to the height of from four to ten feet.

By the time I had returned, on March 4th, the flood was past, and the waters settled down in their old courses. Lieut.-Colonel Herrick had recovered the barrel-punt near the heads at the Waitotara mouth, and, having taken it to pieces, brought the materials back to Poronui, the crossing place below Weraroa, where my headquarters remained. Lieut.-Colonel Lyon had made every preparation for a forward movement with his portion of the force, and on the 5th all the troops resumed the positions they held before the flood, and cleared another mile of road to the front. We had, however, still to make rough bridges and culverts to cross the tributary creeks, which were still swollen and their banks covered with soft mud.

Some eighty Wanganui natives had now joined Major Kemp's selected corps, and with the Arawa Division (No. 8 A. C.) under Captain Gundry and Captain Porter, as a second native column, I felt able to follow the enemy in the bush where Europeans could not be relied upon to find or keep a track. With the certainty of operations in the bush before me this was the best force I could use in this way, though neither the Wanganui nor the Arawa tribe are bushmen in the sense that North American Indians are said to be, nor have they the faculty of following or finding a trail which the "black-fellows" of Australia, or the natives of South Africa, possess to so eminent a degree.

Among the Maoris only two tribes approach the South Africans, the Uriwera and Ngatiporo. The former, though the most expert, were unavailable as they were in rebellion, and sheltering Te Kooti in their fastnesses. The Ngatiporo, however, under their veteran leader Ropata, had no military duty on hand, and I therefore applied for a detachment of that tribe for this special duty. The government approved my suggestion, and an officer had been sent up to select 100 to 150 men out of that numerous tribe.

I must point out how my efforts to procure this reinforcement were obstructed, till too late to be of use, by Mr. McLean, who was on that account removed from the office which he held as government agent. Meanwhile I had resolved to trust my force, composed as it now was chiefly of men who had had some weeks' experience of field and bush life and a Maori contingent.

CHAPTER 8

The Enemy Retreats and Troops Move Forward

On the 7th, therefore, I began my forward movement. The Arawas ascended the range to the right of the bush valley, provisioned for three days, and Captain Gundry in command of them had orders, if he struck Titokowaru trail, to follow and keep it, relying on me for support. Major Kemp took the left ridge, following the road as far as it went, and I accompanied the column. The European force remained at the road with the pack transport, for which they were to continue making the track passable. Kemp had started early, and pushed on so far that it became obvious to me that either the enemy had abandoned this part of the country, or that he was in position towards the line of Captain Gundry's march.

I therefore directed Kemp to return to the Europeans, while taking Nos. 1 and 2 Divisions A. C. with us, we pushed on some miles in Captain Gundry's direction through the bush. At length we reached a native encampment and found traces of the Arawas, who must have passed that morning, and following their trail, which at this point turned to the left, we moved on to support him.

On reaching the summit of the range we discovered that Gundry's trail turned towards the advanced camp of the day before, and I therefore left it and pushed forward myself to endeavour to obtain a better outlook. From a favourable position which was thus gained I was able to examine the whole valley, and, finding no smoke or other indication of the enemy's presence, I assumed that he had been compelled by the recent floods to evacuate this part of the country, and had in all probability retired to or beyond the Patea. I therefore sent back the Europeans and overtook the Arawas who had halted for me. They reported finding a dead Maori, evidently shot in one of the late skirmishes at a rebel camp, and Titokowaru trail in the direction of Okotuku. At this point I knew there was neither shelter nor food, so I assumed as certain he had moved back to the Patea district. This simplified matters, and enabled me to advance with a light heart.

On the 8th, therefore, I reconnoitred to find a good line by Te-ori-ori to Wairoa, and sent Kemp with a strong native column to examine the Okotuku tracks, which resulted in proving the accuracy of the conclusions of the day before, inasmuch as the enemy's trail was soon found, and followed far enough to show that he had retreated beyond Okotuku towards Patea. I therefore directed Lieut.-Colonel Fraser to open out a clear track from the bush towards Wairoa, which would hereafter facilitate movements from that place towards the Waitotara at Papatupu, should these ever be required, while I prepared to move my whole force, stores and material forward to Wairoa, and if possible, to Patea. I had placed Lieut.-Colonel St. John in command at that place, and on my return to Weraroa I received a report from him to the effect that Titokowaru had reached the Patea River, and was in force at Putahi and New Taranaki.

All doubt as to the expediency of resuming my advance being thus dissipated, and as the weather had broken and rain was descending in torrents, Lieut.-Colonel Fraser judiciously hurried his march, crossing a large swamp only just in time to avoid being stopped by its inundation, and arrived with his column at Wairoa. Major Kemp and Captain Gundry and his Arawas returned to Weraroa, and encamped at Perekama, where Lieut.-Colonel Lyon already was with his division and the barrel-punt. I myself went to Wairoa. On the 10th Nos. 1, 2, and 6 Divisions A. C. moved to Norman's Flat, near Wairoa, where before sunset the native column and No. 4 A. C. joined them, escorting the drays with the camp equipage and baggage from Weraroa. I had, however, to send the drays back for stores to Weraroa, and to rejoin me by the beach road, having only about half the number required for a movement of my whole force. Lieut.-Colonel Lyon was ordered to escort the stores next day and rejoin the force with his rear-guard.

Lieut.-Colonel St. John, summoned by me from Patea, arrived at my headquarters at 5 p.m. on the 10th, and reported that some drays he had sent to join me had been attacked by a party of natives from Titokowaru force, which he believed to be encamped on high ground on the left bank of the Patea River. The attack proved of little importance, Lieutenant and Quartermaster Hunter having promptly extended his men, fired upon and charged the enemy, whom he drove off, taking one or two horses and some arms, and inflicting some loss upon him. The flooded state of the river had prevented the drays from crossing the Whenuakura River, but they were halted on the bank. On the 11th I therefore borrowed what drays I could from the Wairoa settlers, and taking the most necessary articles of my camp equipment, I moved to Patea, pitching the tents to seaward of the sandhills, and beyond the view of Titokowaru camp, which was plainly visible, commanding the whole country, and overlooking Patea.

I had ordered all the boats procurable to be hauled across the piece of beach from the Patea to the Whenuakura River, and used them to bring across the men and horses, while, with the drays on the other side of the river, which were dragged through the stream by the men, I finished the removal of my baggage from Norman's Flat. It was a hard day's work, and the rear-guard did not reach Patea till 11 p.m. Meanwhile, the contemplated removal of my reserve ammunition, hospital, and stores, had been interrupted by the weather. I had ordered the drays to proceed by the Waitotara mouth, so as to dispense with a strong escort, but on arriving at that point, they found themselves separated from me by the flooded state of the river, and therefore returned to Weraroa, where I had left a garrison in the redoubt. They were, therefore, unloaded there, and dragged down the hill by the men, their contents being packed down the hill, and were taken across in the barrel punt, as the road was not yet available for loaded drays.

Thus, on March 11th we once more occupied our November positions, and the country from the Whenuakura to the Kai-iwi was again in our possession. I reported at this time to the government that I now proposed to relieve myself of my baggage as soon as possible, and prepare to bring operations to a conclusion by closing, if possible, with the enemy. Titokowaru was almost in the identical position which he had held in October, when I took command, and before his march in the bush round my flank, only he was on the other side of the Patea River. He had uniformly concealed his movements in this manner, and displayed none of that confidence which in the former warfare of the coast had been evinced by the rebel tribes when the royal troops were opposed to them.

At Nukumaru, in 1865, a body of Maoris had penetrated a royal camp and almost reached the general's tent in broad daylight, though their numbers were not equal to our own, yet during all the months that had elapsed since Moturoa, though during the greater part of the time they had been far more numerous and better accustomed to war than our men, and far better armed than those opposed to H. M.'s troops, we could not induce them to attack us, or even to stand their ground in the open. It seemed, therefore, that Titokowaru was resolved not to be forced to fight, and to persist in retreating, as he had advanced, by the bush, in order to confine himself to the Maori traditional warfare of surprise or ambuscades.

During such weather as we had lately experienced, I knew he could not retreat easily in the bush encumbered with women and children in a district traversed by so many easily swollen rivers, which a few hours' rain converted into torrents. All therefore depended on the men and their confidence in themselves. The enemy, if he buried deeper and deeper in the jungle, must be resolutely followed and, even if we could not get to close quarters with him, must eventually be driven out of the district. The total impossibility of obtaining information was a serious difficulty and one which I could only partially remedy.

A small picked body of guides under Sergeant Maling were daily becoming more and more useful, and did much good work in the way of scouting, manifesting both endurance and courage to no small degree. This little corps was limited to fifteen, but so many were the casualties that while I never had more than the fixed number available at one time, quite thirty were enrolled during the few months I held command. For any reconnoitring on a large scale I was dependent on Major Kemp, whose experience, devotion, and courage were from first to last remarkable. My chief danger lay in permitting my newly-raised force to become entangled in unknown and densely wooded spots, where Titokowaru might have prepared ambuscades, or even a *pah*, without our knowledge, from which a few unexpected volleys suddenly poured in might create a panic. The impossibility of flanking a march in a forest so full of undergrowth and supplejack, added much to our risks.

All marches had to be conducted in Indian file, and therefore at no one spot was it possible to have any large force to reply to an ambuscade before the enemy retreated, while the care of the wounded in such a position was very embarrassing. But on the other hand, my force was now greatly improved. Misbehaviour before the enemy was now generally accepted as disgraceful by the public opinion of the men. The ridiculous parapet round the encampments, without which when I took command the troops never could sleep, was a thing of the past. Already the men had practised bivouac life, and the bell tent was no longer indispensable, nor from this turning point of the operations did the men see much more of their tents. The terror of the bush had evaporated and, if our men were still inexpert in getting through it, and if, hampered as they were with blankets, haversacks, ammunition and clothes, they could make but moderate marching, I felt sure a very little experience would induce them to lighten their loads.

There was, however, one crime in the force which did much to destroy the comradeship of the men, and this, together with misbehaviour before the enemy, I considered the time opportune to grapple with. Undoubtedly among the recruits there were many dissipated men, whose conduct a large section of the press held up to constant abuse, and there were also a few blackguards. The men not having, as an English soldier would have, the feeling that his countrymen honoured those who fought their battles, considered that they served purely for money. The necessities of government compelled them to receive their pay much in arrear, but when paid they received considerable sums. There was no way of spending money, so they had to carry it about their persons, and thus it happened that certain rascals were enabled to rob their comrades when asleep or compelled to leave their "swags," to cook or to perform duties.

This crime had become so prevalent and was producing such bad effect among the men that I took steps to have a culprit caught and resolved to make an example. Sub-Inspector Foster, with considerable cleverness, caught a man red-handed, that is to say, with his plunder upon him, and I immediately ordered his trial by general court martial. At the same court I had another prisoner tried on a much graver charge. I have mentioned that Lieutenant Turner had gallantly repulsed an attack upon the escort of the wagons on the 10th inst.

On that occasion, and directly the enemy opened fire, the sergeant seized a horse which was being led by one of the men and, mounting him, galloped away to Wanganui, where he reported himself as the sole survivor of the convoy. I got the leaflet published as an extra by a Wanganui paper that night, and I at once sent in a corporal and two mounted men to make the sergeant a prisoner, and bring him to my headquarters for trial on the capital charge of cowardice and shameful misbehaviour before the enemy.

The court martial sat accordingly, and the offences being proved, sentenced both prisoners to fifty lashes and two years' imprisonment. I sent back the proceedings of that upon the sergeant as being a wholly inadequate sentence, but the officers, perhaps fearing the responsibility of a death sentence, which is supposed to attach rather to the President and members than to the confirming officer, adhered to their decision. If the responsibility does really lie upon the officers composing such a court, I presume that it will always be difficult, however necessary, to make an example even if the prisoner is caught in treasonable correspondence with an enemy. A commander, who must best know when such examples are absolutely required, would be unworthy of his position if he flinched from the responsibility, and I felt this just one of those moments when an example was required. Cowardice till very recently was regarded as a very venial offence in the force and men would even laugh at the most disgraceful behaviour.

A change was now beginning to come over many of the men, and I thought that it was seasonable time to mark the gravity of the crime, and the punishment it involved. However, I could not, as it happened, bring about what I thought so necessary, and while glad in my heart to be absolved from the duty of taking a life, even though doing so might have the effect of preventing future disaster and sacrifice of many lives. I felt the necessity of emphasizing on parade the fact that the punishment awarded was wholly insufficient.

I accordingly had the men fallen in and the thief flogged. The sergeant was tied up, but I only caused him to receive one stripe, as no flogging could make a man brave, nor the fear of it prevent others being cowardly. The one stripe sufficed to stamp his conduct as disgraceful, and I consequently had him then cast loose. In the case of the thief it was different; flogging might, and in fact did, deter the few rascals in the force from following his example, and the bad men were in time discovered and got rid of, in all probability, for other offences.

I warned the officers who formed the court martial that they had not acted in accordance with the Mutiny Act, which by their oath they had been bound to comply with, and that if they accepted service in which certain responsibilities devolved upon them they must bear them or retire; and I informed the men that if the officers did their duty in such cases, I might be relied upon to do mine. Practically I felt sure that after this court martial there would be no further instances of glaring misconduct. By this time the men had acquired a certain military feeling, and it was evident that cowardice was not now looked upon lightly, but with some contempt.

After the punishment parade I ordered rations to be served out, and the whole force to march that night at 8 p.m., with the intention of attacking Titokowaru in his camp.

It is a significant commentary on the effect of politics, that the sergeant tried and sentenced for misbehaviour of the most glaring and shameful kind, was subsequently released by the next government, and restored to his former rank in the force.

I marched in two columns, one of 400, under my own command, by the proper left of the Patea River, to attack Titokowaru at Otautu, and the other 200 strong by the right bank, to intercept his retreat towards "Gentle Annie," under Lieut.-Colonel St. John. Night marches are always wearisome, but though a trifle sleepy, and more or less uncomfortable from being prevented from smoking, the men moved along well, and as the first signs of dawn showed themselves, we surprised the Maori sentinel sound asleep under a bush. I had the Arawas in front, and the moment before had been with the advance, though I had halted just then to look back to see if the rear was keeping up. I always carried in my girdle a Maori tomahawk, a trophy from Ngatapa, and if I had been where I was a moment or two before the sentry would have been noiselessly killed.

As it was the Arawas asked for a tomahawk, and in calling for one they woke the sentry, who sprang to his feet, and, dodging round the bush, escaped, though fired at and wounded, though he was able to give the alarm. There was a thick fog overhanging the hill top, to which probably the sentry owed his escape, which now told greatly against us. It is needless to say I extended and advanced my men at a run as we found evident signs of the proximity of the camp. Colonel Lyon I left with half the force a little behind in reserve till I could observe the position.

The enemy now turned out and fired upon us, several men falling, but we could see nothing. The guides, Arawas and No. 1 A. C., and Kemp's men answered the fire, which they thought came from above, and crept up so near that the enemy's voices could be heard. In such a light neither side could take aim, so the firing, though very heavy, was not very effective, at least upon our men. Moreover, though there was a clearing we were surrounded by a dense bush, in which each side took cover.

Our reserve, under Colonel Lyon, especially the native part, was becoming so excited that they could not be prevented firing at nothing in particular, and was therefore brought up to the front by the officer in command to lessen the risk of our men being shot by the reserve. In a thick jungle it is very difficult to control men when spread out in skirmishing order, without plenty of trained non-com.

officers to supervise them. As we were beginning to lose some men, and could not see a yard away from us, I determined to reconnoitre myself in the bush to my front. Taking therefore a bugler and the chief Kemp and Major Swindley, my *aide-de-camp*, and my interpreter, Captain Preece, I struck out from our right front, and then turned to my left. I found myself descending a hill, and in a few moments at the edge of a clearing, in which men, women, and children were packing up their movables, and as each got loaded making off into the bush.

Turning towards my own force I saw a few of the enemy's skirmishers, and as far as the knees of my men, quite close to them. It was clear that this dense fog was hanging only on the summit of the hill, and that we were in occupation of that summit. A very few feet lower down all was clear. I therefore sounded the advance and double, and the affair was practically at an end. The enemy retreated precipitately, leaving his incomplete bundles, and even in some cases his arms, and made off towards the river.

I had expected this, and hoped Lieut.-Colonel St. John's force was in concealment ready to dispute the ford. To my great disappointment, however, I now heard volleys from a great distance, evidently from the summit of Gentle Annie, too far to be of the smallest use, but showing the enemy that his retreat was cut off in that direction. It was disappointing, as it compelled Titokowaru to strike inland at right angles to the coast line, and made the pursuit more difficult.

Nevertheless, Major Kemp pushed on with his picked men and Arawas, and found some bodies and killed one or two fugitives on the line of their flight. After a lapse of a couple of hours, he returned, bringing in one or two women in order to obtain information. But he had been thrown out by the volleys from Gentle Annie, which had caused Titokowaru to scatter in all directions inland, while he had made his own way down towards the fords at which he had hoped to arrive before the enemy and, consequently, got a bad start. Titokowaru's camp had been occupied, we ascertained, by 400 "guns," but had suffered considerably from desertions. The rebel leader had been present in person, and our attack had been a complete surprise.

It was satisfactory to find that whatever had been the case at the time of Moturoa, now at least for some time there had been no treasonable communication between them and the Wanganui natives, as they were ignorant of many things of importance to them. They were also suffering from the effects of the hardships undergone since they abandoned Taurangahika, and their early dispersion, through *hapus* dropping away one by one into the interior, seemed certain to follow if, while in depressed spirits, they were actively and resolutely pursued. There were some difficulties in the way of a pursuit directly inland, but I felt sure that Titokowaru would change his line of retreat as soon as our force barring his way was removed, and that he would attempt to keep the line of the coast a few miles within the bush. By this means he could supply himself with vegetables, pigs, and fruit at the several bush settlements, or even at those on the verge of the bush which were larger and better provisioned.

Our casualties had amounted to three killed and twelve wounded. Of the latter I regret to say many proved to be mortally wounded, but we were ill-provided for a campaign as regards the hospital and medical department. The wounded I had conveyed to Patea by boat as being less likely to shake them than carriage in stretchers by bearers. The whole force then crossed the Patea, and moving by Manutahi outside the bush, got in front of Titokowaru's probable line of retreat. Meanwhile, on the 15th, Kemp explored the right bank of the Patea, but not finding traces of the enemy, I sent him and the Arawas across the stream again next day to ascertain in what direction Titokowaru was moving. They soon ascertained that he had actually crossed the river at some distance inland and, returning themselves, avoided the broken and difficult country of the Patea banks and re-entered the bush from the open country.

On the 16th Lieut.-Colonel Lyon patrolled the country from Manutahi towards Taumaka, but found no traces of the enemy. I left the force under this officer on this day, and proceeded to Patea to report to government and make final arrangements, as I did not contemplate returning to that post, where my stores of all kinds were kept, till the operations were over.

I had, however, arranged before leaving that Major Kemp's column should be made up to 350 men by bringing up the Wanganui natives, who were not in his own corps, from Patea, to which they had gone without orders after Otautu, and adding sixty European volunteers under Captains Northcroft and Watts. It was a great proof how the Maori chief Kemp had raised himself in the opinion of the force, that officers and men of the Europeans willingly volunteered to serve under his orders. There was now no difficulty in getting volunteers for that service, and in fact a selection had to be made so as to keep the numbers down to those I had fixed upon. I had not expected to hear from Kemp on this day at all, and did not intend to return to camp till next morning.

But, as it happened, at 10 p.m., Lieut.-Colonel Lyon, commanding in my absence, received an urgent message from the chief to the effect that he had discovered the enemy in a *pah* at Whakamara, which had been built some time ago close to the *kainga* on an open space of half a square mile, some distance within the bush, not many miles from Mokoia. Lieut.-Colonel Lyon at once got his men, in all 250 to 300 in number, under arms, and proceeded to reinforce Kemp, using his messengers as guides. Before leaving his bivouac he sent a despatch to inform me of what had occurred and the steps he had taken, and that he had left a detachment of mounted men to escort me if I thought it best to proceed by the open country and make my way next morning to Whakamara by the shorter bush path leading from the Mokoia direction.

Whakamara is situated on an open clearing within the bush, and, though a village which Europeans had rarely been allowed to visit, was nevertheless a well-known Maori settlement. Titokowaru choice of a position so much further to the north showed that he was retreating towards his own country as fast as he was able, and under such circumstances all uncivilized warriors lack the necessary bottom to make a sturdy fight, and become speedily demoralised.

Colonel Lyon therefore acted most judiciously in at once marching, notwithstanding the hour and the difficulties of the bush, much enhanced as they proved to be by the steep chasms he was compelled to pass in the dark. These were the deep beds of streams running perpendicularly to the sea, torn out in times of flood, and were often sheer precipices of rocks on both sides. To get across the natives had made a sort of rough ladder firmly fixed at each end, by which they scrambled down or up the worst of these perpendicular banks.

Colonel Lyon was of course much delayed by these crossings, but he obstinately continued his march through the night. I got back to the camp after midnight, and leaving the horses with a few of the men I found there, I hurried after Colonel Lyon by the line he had taken with a few dismounted men. I caught up the column about daylight entering the open land near Whakamara, having of course been able, by marching light with only a few men, to move much faster than the troops. I had hardly, however, reached the front by the narrow track through fern seven feet high, which shut out all view, when I saw towering above the fern and close by the column a native horseman mounted on a white animal to my left front. He had clearly ridden from the *pah*, which was not far off in the clearing we were traversing, though as yet invisible to us, and owing to the height of the fern he had failed to see our men.

Something, however, attracted his attention about the same moment as I caught sight of him, for he stopped, turned, and fired the six shots of his revolver, not so much caring to hurt us, for he took no aim, as to give the alarm to his friends; then swiftly turning, he galloped away to our right. Our advance fired, but he escaped apparently unwounded. Kemp had meantime preceded the column and reached the bush at the further side of the clearing, and was making his way to get round the *pah* when this untoward occurrence took place. Colonel Lyon hurried on at once, as did Kemp, but Titokowaru would not fight, and beat a precipitate retreat.

We judged from his getting away so quickly he must have been on the point of resuming his march, when he sent out his scout, whom we recognised as the well-known Katene, to see if our troops were moving in his direction. We soon reached the deserted *pah*, and Kemp followed as fast as he could in the direction in which the enemy had made off. But finding themselves pressed, Titokowaru's followers dispersed in all directions, and Kemp had a difficulty in overtaking even a few of the fugitives, whom he shot, as they would neither stop nor surrender.

On the same day, the 18th, leaving Kemp's column to continue the pursuit, we marched back to Mokoia to breakfast. The baggage carts were then moved forward by Turuturu-mokai, and we pitched our camp at Taiporohenui, close to the bush, to await tidings from Kemp.

At Whakamara, Kemp had, before I arrived, distinctly heard a native *tangi* lamenting the losses at Otautu, and Titokowaru haranguing his people and complaining of desertions from his force. As soon as he had cooked, he continued the pursuit, which he had suspended when the enemy dispersed, and at sunset came up with the rear-guard. Titokowaru attempted to lay an ambuscade for him as he approached, but Kemp discovering it, attacked with so much rapidity and determination that the party could not hold its ground, and sprang away after delivering their fire, and dispersed in all directions. The emulation of the Europeans and natives caused the utmost exertion to be made to overtake them, but they escaped with the loss of one killed and, as we subsequently learned, another badly wounded, in the skirmish.

Kemp, however, pressed on, and in spite of having to clamber up a precipice in the bush, once more overtook Titokowaru, who again fled precipitately, abandoning his camp and some of his baggage with his food which was actually being cooked for the evening meal. Throughout this trying night and day work the sixty A. C. European volunteers kept up, though encumbered with their heavy marching order equipment and rations, and at the first shot rushed each time to the front to encounter the enemy. Captain Northcroft, their commanding officer, the favourite hero of the A. C., who had personally distinguished himself in many an encounter, for which, had it then existed, he would have received the New Zealand Cross, won the admiration of Kemp and the native column both by his extraordinary activity and reckless daring.

The high distinction of the Cross had been recently instituted at my instance, and being now available as a reward for individual and remarkable instances of gallantry and devotion, all the force hoped it would ere long decorate this officer's breast. In former years he had been so frequently conspicuous, and in this campaign was showing so much zeal and energy, that we looked upon him as certain to be one of the first selected for the decoration. Nevertheless, though he lost no chance of distinguishing himself either on this memorable expedition of Kemp's or on any other occasion, and although there was no possibility of any occasion which could be quoted as entitling him escaping notice as, from myself to the junior of the force, all desired him to get it, no opportunity actually presented itself of giving him the Cross. In fact, while always prominent, always ready to volunteer or to run any risk, fortune did not again favour him to the end of the campaign.

I record this here, because there are on the roll of the Order many who have not done half as much as Captain Northcroft during their service to deserve the proudest decoration open to a New Zealander, and we, who know him well and appreciate him so highly, feel that the Order would be honoured by counting him among its members.

It was the evening of the 20th when Kemp and his column emerged from the bush at my camp at Taiporohenui, and they were received with acclamation by the troops. The Europeans all seemed in high spirits after their hard work, and Kemp could not find words sufficiently flattering to apply to them. They had surprised the Maoris in getting through the bush, they had tried hard to bring about a definite fight, and had shown that with little practice our race is quite able to hold its own even in the most difficult and longest marches, through a dense jungle absolutely unknown. The Maoris had not been behindhand in carrying out the expedition, though Kemp's admirable plans and indomitable energy had not been rewarded as he hoped by a set engagement.

Mile after mile they had managed to keep the trail, and constantly overtaking the enemy, had burst into his camp, only to be again disappointed by his headlong flight. Over and over again they thought themselves on the point of bringing him to action, but always found that he had flung away his impedimenta, blankets, food, and even arms, to lighten his force in making its escape. Some few they had overtaken and shot since leaving Whakamara, five men in all, and they brought in three women prisoners, from whom they hoped to obtain information for me. It is curious how willing prisoners so taken, of either sex, are to recount all that they know themselves. That Titokowaru was now making the most desperate exertion to extricate himself from that part of the country, and to regain his own, was evident. That he had lost his prestige, and that his force was panic-stricken and demoralised, we easily inferred from the accounts of the women.

Desertion was rife, whole *hapus* were breaking away to perpetual alarms, during some of which they had left things behind in their camps essential to their safety and comfort, such as ammunition, blankets, and food. That they were reduced to great straits, living on the maggots of the matai trees and such vegetable products of the forest as are scarcely edible except when pressed by hunger—these and many other details of that painful retreat were narrated by the women, who appeared worn out with fatigue themselves.

The most valuable intelligence, however, we obtained was that Titokowaru was making for the Ngaire, a swamp a long way in the bush beyond Tito-tiro-moana. On looking at the map of the district, I saw that to gain that point Titokowaru must make a considerable detour unless he came outside or near the edge of the bush. Kemp therefore advised our moving by the open to Keteonetea, and entering the bush beyond that point, so as to anticipate the enemy at the Ngaire. To do this successfully, I should have at once and by forced marches pushed on to this unknown Ngaire, which nobody yet that I could find had ever visited. But Kemp's column was exhausted, and I could get no further than Keteonetea next day, where I then pitched my camp.

I sent a despatch to New Plymouth about this time asking the officer in command to move up towards Ngaire to intercept the enemy's retreat, and I took this occasion to decorate certain men of the force with the ribbon of the newly-created distinction of the New Zealand Cross, which, as I informed them, had been instituted by the queen to reward special acts of valour as a token of the recognition and gratitude of the colony, and the honour in which it held those who were conspicuous in fighting its battles. It is foreign to this memoir to describe the difficulties which arose through Sir George Bowen's having created an Order of Chivalry without reference to the "Fountain of Honour." But in the end Her Majesty was pleased to adopt the Order, and to recreate it as her own, ordaining that it should be granted on the recommendation of ministers in her name by her governor in accordance with the statutes already published in the *Colonial Gazette* of March, 1869.

She furthermore was pleased to declare that it should rank with and next after the Victoria Cross. This decoration I had recommended in order to raise the tone of the force, and to afford some higher inducement than that of mere pay to the officers and men engaged in the arduous duties of the campaign. Lieut.-Colonel Gorton, whom I had despatched to New Plymouth, was specially charged to make contracts for supplies throughout the northern part of the Taranaki district into which I foresaw that my operations must speedily bring my force, as the distance of my base at Patea must otherwise entail inconvenience and expense in land carriage.

All my force now petitioned for a little more time to rest before again entering upon laborious and active operations in the bush. But though I felt they had earned consideration, I recognised that much depended upon pressing the flying remnant of Titokowaru force. There was a probability of reaching the Ngaire before him, and almost a certainty of finding him there even if we could not reach that point the first. I felt sure he would be compelled to halt at the Ngaire to rest awhile, not only to recover from the fatigue his force had undergone, but because it was the last *kainga* at which he could rely on provisions for many days, if he meant to make for the Upper Waitara.

These considerations compelled me to decide upon marching on the 22nd, and I therefore issued four days' provisions at Keteonetea, and moved off with the bulk of my force at 7 a.m. on that day. I left directions with Quartermaster Collins, the able officer in charge of my commissariat and transport, to be prepared to bring up further supplies of ammunition and provisions, if I sent for them, utilising the pack saddles I had purposely provided myself with and carrying them on the backs of Mr. Quinlan's admirable cart horses. Our cart transport was a service which, though hurriedly created, nevertheless could not have been surpassed in the staunchness and quality of its draught animals, and I felt sure that Mr. Collins and Mr. Quinlan would prove quite equal to any demands I might have to make on their activity and zeal.

CHAPTER 9

Capture of Te Ngaire

I resolved this time to accompany Kemp myself, as it was far from unlikely that the operations to be successful might continue for some time, and take us to some district so remote from my camp that it would be necessary either to emerge from the bush in another part of the country, or to make arrangements to procure provisions and have them forwarded from another point of supply. In anticipation of this I had already made arrangements at Taranaki, but transport must have been extemporised if I sent requisitions for supplies; and I felt that, independently of my presence probably keeping the bush expedition in better heart, it was essential that my authority should be available to prevent any miscarriage of the expedition from a want of provisions or other necessary requirements.

We moved therefore on the 22nd, as I have already said: the corps of Kemp, the Arawa Division under its Captain (Gundry) who had re-joined with a few Northern Ngapuhi natives, with the corps of guides and the Europeans. At Tito-tiro-moana we halted the European force under Lieut.-Colonel Lyon, and with, the two native corps and guides I pushed on with Kemp, who showed much aptitude in keeping the trail of the fugitives which we soon struck in the forest. Moving on, we came to more than one spot at which they had rested, one being a camp they had fled from in one of their panics, probably at night, for we found in it clothes, blankets, &c.

We clearly discovered that Titokowaru had caused his followers to scatter after their panic, but Kemp held to the main line of the retreat, and at length as evening fell we reached the far-famed Ngaire swamp and reconnoitred it, or at least as much of the bank as it was safe to examine without risk of betraying our presence.

I now sent back orders to Lieut.-Colonel Lyon to march at daylight, and bring up the European force, whose labour I foresaw would be valuable if I had to bridge the swamp. From Taranaki I now received despatches. A sort of Committee of Public Safety had been permitted to exist there, consisting of the Superintendent of the Province, Mr. Richmond, brother of the Native Minister, Mr. Commissioner Parris, so well-known and distinguished in all native matters, with others whose names I did not know.

My orders I learned were being carried out by the able officer commanding, Major Browne, and a probability existed that the enemy if defeated by me would be intercepted and destroyed by the force under him. But I was informed by Mr. Parris that the Ngaire was a treacherous swamp which had engulfed 500 Waikato warriors, who in former times had attempted to cross it, and I was warned very seriously not to trust my force upon its shaky surface.

I knew Mr. Parris to be a brave man, and I much suspected that in his own case he would not have allowed a tradition of doubtful truth to discourage him. At all events I resolved not to be turned aside myself. The ammunition horses reached me in the afternoon and Lieut.-Colonel Lyon's detachment in the morning. Meanwhile by further despatches I learned that Major Browne, who had most loyally prepared to assist me by intercepting the enemy, had been prevented by the new Plymouth Committee of Public Safety, and I was further informed that Ahitana, chief of the *hapu* which resided at the Ngaire, had been promised not to be molested if he remained quiet, and that if this promise was broken the whole Taranaki tribe would resent it and rise. There are moments in war when a swift decision has to be made, and this was one of them. I had no doubt that, friendly or not, Ahitana was at this moment entertaining the enemy, and to hesitate in pushing on would have been a fatal mistake.

I regretted the loss of Major Browne's co-operation, for he was a brave man well accustomed to Maori war, and almost sure to intercept the enemy if he escaped. But this, after all, might not be necessary if I was fortunate in surrounding and holding Titokowaru, so I cast all doubt to the winds and resolved to proceed, as I had before decided, with my undertaking. The words I used in my despatch describing the rest of this affair I cannot improve upon; they were written at the moment, and I have not heard that they have been challenged by any one present on the occasion.

One incident, however, I may mention. It occurred directly my plans were ready to be accomplished. It was already growing dark, on the 24th, when my *aide-de-camp*, Major Swindley, announced that Lieut.-Colonel Lyon wished to speak to me, and I at once went to meet him at my fire. Lieut.-Colonel Lyon everyone knows was a Bayard in soul, and one of the bravest of men. Nevertheless, he had heard of this tradition of the Waikato men being submerged, and was greatly exercised in mind.

"Colonel," he said to me, "as your second in command I find it to be my duty to warn you that you are about to attempt a very dangerous adventure—500 Waikatos, &c.—and I think it right to say that under such circumstances you should weigh well the risks."

"Colonel," I replied, "so long as I have had the honour to command this force I have never once asked you or anyone to share my proper responsibility. I have called no Councils of War. I have asked absolute obedience, and have compelled it; therefore, I think it hard that I should, on the eve of an attempt which I have carefully thought out and prepared for, be placed in this position. I bear the whole burden of the responsibility; why make it more grievous than it is? Whatever happens you are not open to blame; but as you feel your duty compels you to take this course, I will not neglect it. I shall tomorrow morning meet the enemy. I may be defeated and my force repulsed. If so, I shall not return; and my men may be like sheep without a shepherd. I shall therefore leave you—the second in command—to rally the force and restore order. It will then be your duty."

Poor Lieut.-Colonel Lyon almost burst into tears. He begged me not to do this, but to let him share the perils and glory of the day. That he had only offered a word of caution, &c. I knew him so well, and esteemed him so highly, that I would not take offence at what he had said, so I passed it over, for I believe he had done violence to his own personal feelings in blurting out what he thought it his duty to say, but which after my remarks he saw was out of place and ungenerous to me. Had the result been as definite and as bloody as we expected, Colonel Lyon would either have been one whose name history would have recorded with honour as one of the most valiant of those who fell for New Zealand, or he would have added fresh laurels to a reputation second to none in the annals of this unfortunate and unnatural colonial civil war.

I resume the story of Te Ngaire from my despatch of March 26th, 1869, dated Taiporohenui.

The swamp, perhaps in winter time a lake, is a rush morass

LIEUT.-COL. LYON, N.Z.M.

with *toe-toe* growing on it here and there along its edges. The bank opposite to that on which I first struck it was apparently that of a promontory or island, of which the side nearest to me was cleared, and on it three large *kaingas* were clearly visible. I did not doubt that I had Titokowaru and his fugitive force before me, and nothing but the physical difficulty of passing the swamp to prevent my at once attacking him. However, as I wished to be prepared to overcome the difficulty, I had brought up Lieut.-Colonel Lyon and the Europeans to assist me if labour was required. This reinforcement reached me at 11 a.m. on the 23rd.

During the night of the 22nd I had caused the swamp to be reconnoitred by a few natives, and ascertained that the surface was really as treacherous as described, and that in places near the southern bank, by the time the enemy had apparently taken, only a very few of the men at a time could pass, without danger. As I felt that in that case, I could not justifiably attempt a surprise unless the opposite shore could first be seized and held, I resolved to wait a day and search for a more favourable spot. All the morning of the 23rd was devoted to this object, and I at last decided to send a party across in advance from a spot some hundred yards from an *eel-weir* (weir) where the swamp was narrowest, to gain the bank and erect an entrenchment while, with hurdles or ladders, I enabled the main body to cross the swamp, without sinking the regular track.

All the next day the armed constabulary worked hard, and constructed a sort of light hurdle ladders of long poles, joined by supplejack twinings and cross sticks. As soon as it grew dark, Major Kemp sent out a party of scouts to explore the swamp, but they failed to find the line used by the natives in coming to their *eel-weirs*. For that day I was therefore compelled to abandon the attempt. Next day, the 24th, I resolved to cross from the *eel-weirs*, giving up my intention of sending two parties; I therefore caused the natives to clear a track in the bush in that direction to enable us to "hump" our hurdles to the bank, while I sent back the Europeans to clear a better road to my camp for the pack horses I had sent for with further provisions. Towards evening all the hurdles were carried to the *eel-weirs*, which were about a mile from the main track I had used in my march.

Ever since reaching the swamp the troops had been strictly prohibited from lighting fires by day, and only permitted to make very small ones at night. The utmost quiet was kept, and every man cautioned not to expose himself to view. The enemy apparently took no precautions, and seemed wholly unsuspicious of our proximity. Yet, we were separated by so short a distance that we distinctly heard a man cry out, "Now this evil man will cause the Wanganuis to come down upon us"—a speech we attributed to one of Ahitana's men, living peaceably at the Ngaire, and who, having refused to join Titokowaru, feared that they might suffer from his being there. The "Evil Man" being, as we felt sure, Titokowaru, our surmises became convictions that he was there. Opinions, however, seemed to differ at the *kainga*, for later on we heard a woman call out, "*Haere mai, haere mai te toa—haere mai ki te kai,*" ("Come hither, come hither the brave—come hither to the food").

We could also clearly perceive that the natives were carrying timber, evidently for a *pah*, which seemed to indicate an intention of remaining and defending their position.

At nightfall on the 24th I passed fifty Wanganui and Arawas, under Sub-Inspector Gundry, across the swamp from the *eel-weirs*, and till 11 p.m. the whole of the natives were employed in carrying the hurdles, and placing them on the line across the swamp. The Europeans then marched up, and while they were divesting themselves of their trousers, and arranging their pouches on their shoulders the natives crossed without accident or noise. The Europeans carried extra ladders to fill up gaps, and in their turn effected the passage of the swamp, the last arriving at the head of the bridge at 4 a.m. on the 25th. I now had all the earlier arrivals silently awakened, and leaving Lieut.-Colonel Lyon with the last comers to hold the bridge head, and act as a reserve to secure our retreat in case of necessity, I moved on through the bush carefully and without noise.

It was growing daylight when we reached the *kainga*, the force being so disposed as to surround it, as it infallibly would have done but for a most unfortunate occurrence. The Maoris of the *kainga* perceiving us rose, and many began to make off; others, however, ran towards us crying out, "*Haere-mai,*" and holding out a white flag, while those apparently escaping hesitated, and seemed disposed to return. At this moment we discovered Kawana Paepae and Aperaniko, two friendly chiefs, and Mr. Booth, R.M., among the natives before us, and I was embarrassed what to do, especially as those escaping seemed many of them to be women. I therefore myself ran down to Mr. Booth at the *kainga*, and was met by Ahitana's son, who protested that those in front of me were all either his own people, or another neutral tribe from Oraukuku, a place I had never heard of before. I therefore asked him why he was preparing a *pah*, and he replied plausibly, that he feared as Titokowaru was "broken" he might be in danger from his pursuers. He admitted the speech we had heard about the "evil man," and said it referred to Titokowaru, who had crossed the swamp three days before.

Meanwhile, those sent by me to surround the *pah* had halted, and people were creeping, and had crept away by the edge of the swamp, but Tukerangi (Ahitana's son) undertook to bring them back, and sent a man with one of mine for that purpose. As these continued absent, and Mr. Booth had discovered from a seemingly half-witted old man that Titokowaru and his people, or some of them, had been at the *kainga*, I despatched No. 8, the Arawa Division A. C., to bring in the people who had fled. Unfortunately, nearly an hour had been lost when the Arawas started in pursuit, and as we had seldom been able, with an hour between us, to overtake fugitives, or even come up with the women, and as they were travelling light, having abandoned their food and baggage, the pursuit of the Arawas was fruitless. The trail lay towards Te Ngutu, and was followed to the track of General Chute's march.

It would be vain to attempt to describe the vexation and disappointment of the force, which, after overcoming the difficulties of disguising its presence by so much self-denial and privation, and after bridging and passing the swamp unperceived, believed itself to have been duped out of its reward. The only consolation was that even at the price of losing our opportunity we had kept faith with Ahitana, on whose neutral or friendly disposition it was said that of the Taranakis depended, and who, being closely related to the Wanganuis, they felt great sympathy for.

It was not much use cross-examining Tukerangi, as circumstances momentarily proved that the escapees were in fact the enemy we were in search of, but for what it was worth I did so. He said Titokowaru meant "to die on his own land" at the Ngutu, where he then was. He admitted, however, that ten of the enemy, whose names he gave, had been at the *pah* when I arrived, but that he had been afraid to tell me so.

I felt great distrust of this young man and his followers, and a strong inclination to disarm them, and make them prisoners. But I refrained, insisting only that he should show me Titokowaru trail across the swamp. This he undertook, but as he failed to do so I ordered him and his people, under pain of their neutrality being thenceforward disregarded, to remove to Keteonetea, where they have another *kainga*, and could be under observation. I disbelieved his statements, and felt sure that the women we saw and the men making off were Titokowaru, whose rear-guard at least, if not he himself, had slept the night at Te Ngaire.

Circumstances soon proved that my surmise was right. We at once explored Te Ngutu, which had clearly not been occupied for months, and it was elicited from Ahitana's followers in the course of the next few days that all Titokowaru remaining force and he himself had been at the *kainga* when we came up.

I now withdrew my force to Waihi, where I was joined by Wickliffe (Wikiriwhi), the Ngatiporo chief, and a reinforcement of nearly 100 of his tribe. I felt sure active hostilities in the Patea district were over, and I therefore dismissed the Wanganui natives to their homes. From two of Titokowaru women among the Ngaire natives I learned many details of the enemy's retreat. Seventy of Titokowaru people, and all his women, except those whose weakness had succumbed to the fatigues, were at the Ngaire when I surprised it, and subsequently made off to the upper Ngatimaru district.

No organised enemy therefore remained, and I resolved to move on to New Plymouth, to ascertain whether a rumoured invasion by the Ngatimaniapoto tribe from Mokau had any probability. The Ngatiporo, wholly unconnected with the natives of the West Coast, and admirable bushmen, I left to patrol the country, and intercept any straggling parties attempting to re-enter it.

A sufficient force under Lieut.-Colonel Lyon, whom I proposed to leave in command, I left to guard Patea itself, and form a nucleus for the defence of the district. With the rest I moved in two columns round Mount Egmont, the one to take ship at Opunake, the other to march round the back of the mountain to the Waitara. This latter force, marching on April 5th, easily reached Mataitawa on the afternoon of the 8th by General Chute's track. No enemy was encountered, nor did anything of any importance occur. A single dead Maori was found on the track who had apparently perished from inanition, while endeavouring to make good his escape to his home with an open bullet wound. Lieut.-Colonel St. John commanded the right column, and reported the road behind the mountain an easy one of not more than forty-five miles.

The left column with the drays, ammunition, baggage, &c., marched on the same day towards Opunake, where, on the 7th, the troops and baggage were embarked on board the *Sturt*, I myself riding on to New Plymouth, where I arrived on the 8th. The drays I sent back to Patea under a native escort. The Hon. Mr. Richmond was at New Plymouth, and on the 9th I accompanied him to Waitara, where all my force was assembled. Thinking it desirable to examine the coast, though disbelieving the rumoured invasion from Mokau, we decided to reconnoitre the coast in the s. s. *St. Kilda*. We examined the beach closely, and found no trace of an enemy, and, arriving at the mouth of the Mokau, fired some shells in the direction of the native *kainga*, without discovering any but a few native inhabitants.

After considering the subject with Mr. Richmond, it was agreed that the danger on the West Coast was no longer pressing, and that the troops should be moved by the government steamers to the Bay of Plenty. Arrangements were therefore made to make the West Coast safe, some of the A. C. being left—one division at New Plymouth, another at Patea, and the Ngatiporo Division (No. 9) at Waihi.

I wrote now to the government to explain my views. I confidently assured them that the war on the West Coast, which had lasted more than nine years, was over, and that nothing remained to be done except to secure the persons of the several fugitive *hapus* by means of systematic search and pursuit by small parties.

It is said to be unwise to prophesy. The war, greater when I arrived than in the days of the royal generals, has never since been re-ignited, and no single pistol-shot in anger has been fired by the tribes.

I am not, therefore, ashamed to recall my forecast on leaving the coast that active rebellion was at an end. Peace has ever since been undisturbed, and if the fanatic Te Whiti did for a time cause considerable alarm, the narrow escapes of the Ngaire and Otautu, the terrible sufferings of the retreat from Waitotara, were still unforgotten, and prevented an outbreak. I say this on the authority of those whose long residence entitles them to rank as experts, and who, in 1879, told me that Titokowaru had constantly declared that he would not fight, even though to maintain his position with his tribe he might make "bouncing" speeches.

Mr. Bryce, participator in the war of 1868-9, acted rigorously in 1881, and perhaps the restless may have been cowed by the force he displayed. But Te Whiti had few arms and little ammunition, and used every effort to restrain the ardour of his followers. For well he knew, and better still Titokowaru, that though the red coats of Her Majesty were no longer to be seen, another set of men, who fought as well, but who were more careless of appearances or forms and less ceremonious in their dealings, were still in the colony, and that before them they could not stand an hour, and that these men now knew their country better than themselves.

Major Noake and Captain Kells, who raised a veteran company, and Lieut. Bryce most actively carried out the programme I had left to be followed by the troops on the coast, and by their gallant exertions the whole Papakohe tribe was at length brought to Patea and placed under guard. The Ngatiporo, who terrified the Ngatiruanui, soon compelled the Tangahoe to surrender to our loyal chief, Hone Pihama, and having given up their arms were practically prisoners on parole. The Waitotaras, fearing to fall into the hands of Noake, Kells, and Bryce, retreated into the interior, and one month after I left, Taranaki settlement had resumed its ordinary aspect.

After Te Ngaire it was safe to ride unarmed from Patea or Wanganui to New Plymouth and, as far as outward appearances went, the great blessing of peace had once more been restored to that long suffering district, by the operations from February 4th to April 12th, 1869. This since 1860 had never really existed, though for some months in 1867 a lull, precursor of a worse storm than any known before, had been too eagerly welcomed as the forerunner of a permanent peace.

CHAPTER 10

The Uriwera Campaign

Accident prevented a very excellent opportunity of meeting with Te Kooti. During the West Coast operations, he had not been idle, and had made another raid on the coast, this time at Whakatane, in the Bay of Plenty. Here he again left traces of blood, and escaped almost with impunity. Major Mair pursued, but his Arawa contingent misbehaved and could not be induced to follow into the Uriwera Mountains. Emboldened by this success, Te Kooti then crossed the mountains to Wai-kare-moana and thence, leaving Wairoa to the north, surprised and killed several settlers and many friendly Maoris at Mohaka, some seventy miles north of Napier.

I had resolved to steer north or south from Waitara, according as the wind was favourable either way, and as it happened to be a south-west wind, made for Manukau, marching across to Auckland and embarking there for Tauranga. Had the wind been from the north, I should have been off Napier on the very day Te Kooti was at Mohaka, and might have landed and attacked his force while carousing at the public house they had plundered, and incapable of resistance or escape.

But in two days he was gone back to the fastnesses of the Uriwera and the chance was lost. We reached Matata by land from Tauranga, and began establishing our depot at that inhospitable spot, for our projected expedition to the Uriwera Mountains. We found a district inhabited only by Maoris, without even enough cattle or sheep to supply the force with meat. There was no shelter for our stores, and apparently no road to the interior for the transport of supplies.

Having discussed the position with Mr. Richmond, who had once more come to acquaint me with the wishes of the government, and to lend me his valuable assistance, I came to the conclusion that we could do nothing by awaiting Te Kooti outside the mountains, because to do so we must have divided our forces in several settlements and left him to choose the most favourable point of attack. True strategical policy demanded our entering the mountains by the best-known paths, and destroying all the food that might be growing or stored at the several native settlements. This course I thought must compel Te Kooti to leave the mountains, where he could with difficulty be attacked except at a disadvantage, and oblige him to come out towards the open country of the interior, where he could be more easily and satisfactorily dealt with.

But the difficulties of such an expedition were enormous. To begin with, the country was almost unknown and, even by examining persons who knew parts, and collating the information thus obtained, it was not easy to get a satisfactory knowledge of the ground. Moreover, it was known that horses could not be taken, or if taken, part of the way could not be fed, and would greatly impede the force. The winter, too, was almost upon us, and the cold of that high region would make it a painful service for the men. Lastly, the base of supply at Matata was most imperfectly divided, and difficult of access. The *Sturt* it is true had come in, but nothing short of the devotion and enterprise of Captain Fairchild could have accomplished this dangerous feat with her.

But it had to be done. Difficulties surround all enterprises, and it is only the weak-minded who shrink from them. Our force now was reliable and inured to hardship, and I felt every confidence in its efficiency. A sort of a map was at length constructed by Mr. Richmond and myself from all the different accounts we could get and the diary of a journey undertaken some years before by Mr. Hunter Brown—the only really reliable account existing. From this map I made my plans and decided to enter the Uriwera Mountains from the three main entrances, and rendezvous if possible, at Ruakituna on the same day.

Accordingly, I divided the force at my own disposal into two columns: the one to enter from Whakatane, the other from the western side at the spot subsequently named Fort Galatea, which was obviously the most important strategical point of the Rangitaiki Valley. The supply of the Whakatane force under Colonel St. John was comparatively easy, as it could be carried out by sea, and the road intervening between the mountains and the coast was practicable and not very long. But to penetrate the country from Ngatata obliged us to depend upon a boat service for some twelve miles up the Rangitaiki River, and upon pack-transport for two days beyond. These services were organised as speedily as possible, boats being brought from Tauranga, and horses hired from the natives. Meat was obtained by sea from Napier; Captain Fairchild having brought two shiploads of sheep which, with difficulty, were forwarded to the interior. In spite of the difficulties to be overcome, great as they appeared, no price seemed too high to pay to dislodge an enemy from a stronghold which was a standing menace and constant danger to the whole of the coast settlements from Matata to Napier.

The Whakatane column under Colonel St. John was composed of 250 Europeans and 140 friendly coast natives. That from Fort Galatea under Major Roberts of 100 Europeans and 200 Arawas, and the third which Mr. Richmond undertook to forward from Wai-kare-moana was to be under the command of Colonel Herrick and to consist of such a force as, in addition to 100 A. C. sent there by me, and the Ngatiporo under Ropata, could be collected in the district.

When, in spite of various delays and bad weather, the two Bay of Plenty columns were ready to start, that by Fort Galatea had to march two days before the Whakatane force. No hitch, however, occurred, and Fort Galatea was occupied and entrenched on May 3rd.

On the 4th and 5th both columns marched, carrying six days' provisions, with a further supply of bacon, borne on the backs of the friendly natives. These latter also carried a certain quantity of spare ammunition.

It is not easy now to understand the immense terror which the Arawas had of the mountains of the Uriwera. They had in times past so often penetrated those defiles and returned decimated and defeated that they could hardly conceive a successful issue to our expedition. Their superstitious dread extended to the neighbouring tribes, and even to the Europeans, but happily had but little influence upon the field force. It was on the 5th that all was ready at Fort Galatea, and our men, loaded with six days' food, moved on. The native bearers carried each of them forty pounds of bacon or 400 rounds of ammunition, for the horses were left behind. We had secured a guide, in whom we had a doubtful confidant, to show us the path, but we trusted to the information we had collected and felt comparatively sure of finding our way.

The first settlement before us, Te Whaiti, was easily found, and we surprised it at early dawn, on the 6th, killing six of the Uriweras and capturing a considerable number of women and children. Here we halted for the night, Mr. Clarke, the R.M., who had kindly accompanied the column, advising this concession to the Arawas who were loath to march forward that day. It was not much better at first, next day, for after waiting till 11 a.m. for them, Major Roberts moved on, taking with him the chief Pokiha (Fox). Ultimately Mr. Clarke brought up the Arawa, and the whole force pushed on towards Ruatahuna. Time was of great importance because Colonel St. John depended upon the support of Major Roberts' column, and a day's rain might at any moment render the road impassable. This lay along the bank of a river between two steep ranges and often by its bed, the river itself being crossed no less than fifty-five times during the day by the column.

The march was necessarily conducted with the greatest caution, for in the narrow defile every yard presented facilities for ambuscade. The corps of guides led the way in single file it being quite impossible, owing to the density of the undergrowth, to provide flankers for the column. At length the march was interrupted and the enemy opened fire from an ambuscade. But the guides, gallantly led by Captain Swindley, A.D.C., and Sergeant Maling, dashed forward, and being at once supported by the leading men of the A. C. column drove off their assailants after a smart skirmish.

In this trifling affair we lost three guides, one mortally and two severely wounded. Hemi, the man mortally wounded, was a native who had served in former years with the 43rd Light Infantry with great credit as a guide. The other two were Europeans, and very valuable members of the force. We were compelled by this delay to halt on the ground where the attack occurred, some two hours' march from the spot at which we had intended to encamp, which was unfortunate, as it retarded our arrival next day at Ruatahuna.

At night the "big mouthed" Arawas whom this skirmish had frightened, entertained us by loudly expressed threats of returning next day; but Fox, their chief, undertook to bring them on after a violent harangue in which he denounced their pusillanimous behaviour. This tribe never so good in action as in boasting before the event, had been spoiled in the past from having formed the majority of all the expeditions with which they had served. Time after time their flinching had rendered each operation in which they took part abortive, but now finding that we were not dependent on them they became more amenable to reason, and at length Fox reported that if permitted to advance at the head of the column, firing as they went at nothing in particular, he could guarantee the good behaviour of his tribe.

On the following morning we sent back a native escort with the wounded and Mr. Clarke, who had fallen lame from an old wound. There was no longer any prospect of concealing our advance, the firing of the previous evening and during the night (for the Arawas fired incessantly, at nothing, to keep their courage up) having echoed through the mountains and given full notice of our approach. I therefore made no objection to Fox's ridiculous proposal.

On the 8th, Fox moved on at the head of the column, firing away briskly, but not hesitating in his advance. The road, after continuing at the bottom of the wedge-shaped ravine along which we had hitherto marched, now turned off to the left and led us up a succession of exceedingly steep ranges, till at 2 p. m. when the summit was gained, at a deserted *pah* called Takuaroa, overhanging the Whakatane River, which flowed closely along its base. There we came in sight of Ruatahuna, which Colonel St. John at that moment was attacking but which, owing to the precipitous nature of the hill, it was plain we could not reach in time to intercept the fugitives. This high mountain, said by Mr. Hunter Brown to be 1300 feet from its base, is almost a precipice, and it would be a good day's work for any man to scale it, even without a load on his back.

But, stimulated by the desire to aid the other force, the men, notwithstanding loads, made great efforts to descend, and Fox's Arawas pushed on with wonderful alacrity. Running, rolling, tumbling, sliding along, at last we got to the foot of the hill, and there, Fox decided to remain, and no persuasion would move him. Swiftly as we had scrambled down, the descent occupied nearly four hours. The Europeans not having come up, and as it was absolutely necessary to communicate, I went forward myself with my staff, a bugler and two of the guides. As evening was past, and night closing in, we had to use a candle to keep the track till we reached the ford of the Whakatane opposite to Ruakituna. Here I directed the bugler to sound the officers' call, and the instant reply, and prolonged cheering of Colonel St. John's force soon showed how baseless had been Fox's alarm, that the armed party might prove to be Te Kooti's force.

Mr. Preece, afterwards R. M. at Napier, then my interpreter, happened a year or two later to revisit the spot with an Uriwera who had been present. It seems that an ambuscade had been set close to the ford, which we passed within a few feet, but when the bugle sounded, the men in ambush, fancying that all our force was at hand, and that they might be caught between the two expeditions, took a sudden panic and made off. Their surprise when Mr. Preece told them the chance they had lost was extreme, but they good-naturedly laughed at their own timidity. From Takuaroa heights we had had a splendid view of the far-famed Uriwera Mountains stretched out before us like a panorama. Nothing but a succession of steep, almost precipitous, forest-clad hills could be discovered all round us, cleft here and there by narrow gullies.

Far away to the eastward were pointed out to us the stony peaks of Tamai-kowha's *pah* at Maunga-powhatu. Towards the north-east were the heights overhanging the entrance of the Waimana and Whakatane Valleys. To the south, the narrow gorge leading by the snowy mountain of Huirau to Lake Wai-kare-moana. Beneath and before us lay the basin in which the central *pah* of Ruatahuna was built—the only spot in which a hundred acres or so of comparatively level land could be descried. This *pah* was fortified, and several small *kaingas* were in its vicinity. But of open and cultivated land there was almost no extent at all visible elsewhere. Here and there a small patch of clearing could be seen, and several others overgrown with scrub which had served as potato patches in former years. About Ruatahuna itself there were larger cultivations than in any other place, but the area was very limited, and insufficient for the support of any large number of natives.

From this circumstance, and from others that came under our observation, two things appeared certain, that the population of the mountains was far from numerous, probably under 300 adult males, and that the amount of food available could not possibly suffice for any considerable demands in addition to the requirements of the tribe. I had calculated upon this, and felt sure that if we could destroy the greater portion of the potatoes and other native food, much of which was not yet harvested, Te Kooti's exodus to the interior would become a question of weeks.

At Ruatahuna the enemy, though in some force, made but a poor resistance. They knew they were between two fires, for Fox's musketry must have been heard since early dawn, and news of the skirmish of the preceding evening had reached them. All their plans for defence had been made on the assumption that Major Roberts' force would arrive first, and it would have done so but for the early halt of the 7th. The road was prepared, and clear lines cut through the scrub in convenient spots to rake an advancing column, or to fire upon it when crossing streams or likely to be stopped by fallen trees.

But Colonel St. John's arrival on the scene, before the sister column made its appearance, disconcerted the Uriwera plans, and left them no resource but flight, except the defence of the *pah*, a kind of warfare for which their habits unfit them, and which could not have been carried out without the certainty of ultimate defeat.

Ruatahuna, though fortified, was really not strong and, when both columns united, could have easily been invested and taken. Of all natives the Uriwera are the least disposed to act in concert in war, each man preferring to fight on his own account, with the free mountains as his refuge if driven back. To have shut themselves up in a *pah*, like rats in a trap, was not only distasteful, but in point of fact must have been fatal to them. They therefore made off in every direction and, from the summits of the surrounding hills, watched the proceedings of the invaders.

Lieut.-Colonel St. John had marched from the Whakatane Valley at Opuriao on the 4th, and on the 5th camped at the foot of the Wharau mountain, where he was joined by his native contingent of 140 men, with thirty-five native bearers. His European force consisted of 250 men, and he had under his command Lieut.-Colonel Fraser, A.C., and Major Mair, R.M., both experienced officers. On the 6th he surmounted the Wharau mountain and surprised the *kainga* of Omarateangi, killing six of the Uriwera. Following the deep valley of the Whakatane River, on the 7th he fell in with an ambuscade at the foot of a hill called Hakeumi, where he lost a gallant officer, Lieutenant White, in charge of the guides, who, though wounded the day before, continued to render valuable service.

The Uriwera had intended to make a stand at this spot, having posted men on a neighbouring hill, as well as on the top, to support the ambuscading detachment. But Lieut.-Colonel St. John turned the flank of the position and carried the hill, in spite of the resistance he encountered and the extreme difficulty of inducing the native contingent to advance. Having gained the summit of the hill without further difficulty, and having halted a short time to cook, he resumed his march and advanced to within 600 yards of Takora, the *pah* of Whenuanui, one of the most influential of the Uriwera chiefs. To have moved directly on Takora would have cost many lives, as the interval was comparatively open, and the troops would have been exposed to the fire of the concealed ambuscading parties of the enemy. Lieut.-Colonel St. John therefore divided his force and moved round both flanks of the *pah* by the bush, a manoeuvre which caused the enemy to evacuate the position.

On the 8th the march was resumed through the bush under considerable difficulties, and about 11 a. m. the force came in sight of Patahoata at Ruatahuna, the *pah* of Pairau, another influential chief of the

Uriwera. Here the enemy made a stand, and Lieut.-Colonel St. John disposed a portion of his force to cover his advance upon the fortification. The enemy had posted a party to threaten the flank of his advance from the bush, and the detachment sent in this direction became hotly engaged when it reached their position.

Meanwhile Colonel St. John, having got within a very short distance of the *pah*, was about to throw up an entrenchment, when the occupants suddenly made off, withdrawing their flanking party and retreating too swiftly to be overtaken by Captain McDonnell who was sent in pursuit. It was during this engagement that Major Roberts' column had reached Takuaroa, and were struggling down the precipitous descent, vainly trying to be in time to intercept the enemy's retreat. During the skirmish on the flank of the *pah* a very fine young officer, Sub-Inspector Travers, scorning to take cover, was mortally wounded in leading his men.

The two columns had thus met with very similar obstructions, although that under Lieut.-Colonel St. John encountered a resistance at Ruatahuna in which that under Major Roberts had not taken part. The loss of Lieut.-Colonel St. John's force, comprising two officers and three men killed and six men wounded, had been more severe, but the total casualties were much less than had been anticipated.

The columns united at Ruatahuna on the 9th, and foraging parties were at once despatched to collect food, and destroy cultivations in every direction.

Meanwhile there was no sign of Colonel Herrick's column which had been expected from Wai-kare-moana, where Te Kooti was believed to be at the time. The Native Minister had relieved me of the care of this column, and had himself proceeded to Napier to organise and push it forward. Lieut.-Colonel Herrick was an officer whom I knew and trusted, and I felt sure that no ordinary obstacle would have delayed him. Except to take part in these operations there was no pressing urgency for an expedition from the Wairoa side, and I felt sure Mr. Richmond would have exhausted every expedient to expedite the march of the column. It was therefore with great anxiety that I watched the gorge leading to Waikare, looking for some sign of our missing column.

Combined operations are always liable to miscarry; in fact, it but rarely occurs where good roads exist and the country is well known, that two expeditions setting out from distant points meet, with anything like punctuality, as the two columns met at Ruatahuna, at a preconcerted place of rendezvous.

That Lieut.-Colonel Herrick might therefore be a day or even two days behind would not have surprised me, but as time went on, I began to fear that he had met with a reverse and had been unable to force his way through to join me. I could, however, only hope for the best, and hold my force ready to lend him support should his approach he ascertained.

The main object of the expedition was the destruction of the food supply in the mountains, and in carrying out this service the troops were aided by the season and the wild pigs. Every potato garden was securely fenced, and the removal of a small portion of the enclosure insured the co-operation of the troops of pigs running in the forest. By next morning in every case the whole of the ground was turned over by the animals, and all the potatoes they did not devour were spoiled by the heavy frosts which occurred every night. A few cattle were found and shot for consumption by the men, and in some instances stray Uriweras, endeavouring to drive them off, were killed by the foraging parties.

So hopelessly had the native inhabitants lost confidence in themselves and their fastnesses that they did not attempt to molest the foragers or combine to avenge themselves on the invaders, but scattered in small groups, occupied the hill tops, and made the mountains resound with their sorrowful *tangis* and lamentations. Yet no opportunity of inflicting loss upon their enemy could have been more suitable to their mode of warfare, and the conformation of the ground, than the ambuscading of these detachments, especially after they had gained confidence from impunity and had ceased to look for resistance.

Nothing could have more clearly demonstrated the conviction which had come home to these mountaineers that they were, at least, on this occasion bearded in their strongholds by a force and by men of whom they had had no experience in their own time and against whom they felt it useless to apply the tactics of their ancestors.

The mountains and the defiles upon which they had relied had failed them this time, and such ambuscades as they had laid had been insufficient to stop or even materially delay the march of their enemy, who was now rioting about among their plantations, apparently quite careless of their proximity. All this tended to convince me that Te Kooti had not yet come upon the scene, for he would have made himself felt long ago, and I therefore expected his approach hourly. The 9th and 10th passed thus; and a slight skirmish occurred on the latter day which resulted in nothing. On the 11th, however, it seemed necessary to make a reconnaissance in force towards Lake Wai-karemoana, in the hope of gaining news of Colonel Herrick's column or falling in with Te Kooti's force. A column was accordingly prepared for this service when Te Kooti's advanced guard came in sight on the top of a hill overhanging the gorge leading from Waikare.

Fox's Arawas to the number of 100 men, supported by 100 of the A. C., under Major Roberts, moved down towards the gorge, and Fox met and drove back the enemy in fine style, leaving a party of men in ambuscade before retiring. Te Kooti's men once more advanced, but the leading man was shot and, thereupon, Te Kooti recalled his force by bugle sound. For what reason it is difficult to say, unless frightened by the unusual sound of an enemy's bugle, the Arawa ambuscade, thereupon, precipitately decamped, and the opportunity of inflicting loss was lost. Fox evidently expected an immediate attack by Te Kooti in force, for he now drew in his lines and joined the A. C. camp, declining to hold his old position some 200 yards lower down the valley.

But no attack was made, and the afternoon and night passed quietly. On the 12th I had hoped to push on further towards the lake, but as too often had been the fate of colonial officers commanding a mixed force of Europeans and natives, I was obliged to be satisfied with a partial execution of my plans. I confess that in my want of information as to the nature of the ground to be traversed, and in my ignorance of the reason of the continued delay of Colonel Herrick's column, I had many doubts as to the advisability of pressing much further into an unknown region, even with willing troops. My supplies were exhausted, and the troops were being maintained on such meat, pigs, cattle, and horses as we could capture, and upon potatoes. The latter though plentiful were bulky and burdensome, and the force could hardly carry more than two days' supply on a march.

I had husbanded my reserve ammunition, and still had a supply on hand, but a single engagement might reduce it materially, for the natives cannot be controlled in their expenditure of cartridges. I was compelled, if I moved forward with a portion of the force, to hold Ruatahuna, both for the sake of the wounded and because in the event of a retreat, unless held by us, the enemy would have been enabled to make such dispositions as to render the ascent of Takuaroa, or in fact any progress beyond Ruatahuna almost impossible.

I resolved, therefore, if I could rely on the support of the native allies both in holding the present camp till our return, and in advancing towards Waikare, that I would make the attempt and be guided by the difficulties I encountered in pushing through to the lake or returning to my camp.

Consequently, I spoke to the natives, and told them what I contemplated but, with the exception of Fox, all the Arawa chiefs opposed the scheme, Petera Pukuatua positively refusing to co-operate. The coast natives throughout had been kept with difficulty from desisting *en masse*, so all depended on the Arawa. When the column moved off, the native portion left their blankets behind, so it was evident we could not go far that day. The Arawa were directed to make a circuit by the left, while the A. C. moved forward by the direct track to the hill where again Te Kooti's force was displaying itself.

Once more upon our approach the enemy made off, leaving a picquet or rear-guard to delay our advance. Major Mair with a few natives had got in front of the Europeans as they pushed on beyond the crest of the hill, and he was fired upon by this picquet and one of the natives slightly wounded, when all but one of his men fell back. But Major Mair, though left almost alone, rushed forward and fired all the charges of his revolver at the enemy before it was possible for them to reload.

Upon this, the picquet seeing the A. C. coming up to Major Mair's assistance, made off precipitately, and were closely pursued. Lower down the hill the Arawas, who had by this time turned the position, reached the main track just as the enemy's picquet ran past, and dashed on in pursuit, inflicting some loss. Petera Pukuatua, who in Fox's absence through illness commanded the Arawa contingent, barbarously cut off and brought back the heads of three of Te Kooti's men who were known and recognised, and others were wounded or killed in the affair.

The Arawa and A. C. had continued their pursuit some miles down the valley, and only halted when they saw the main body of the enemy at a considerable distance, if not entirely beyond our reach. Thereupon, both Europeans and natives returned and made their report, as night was approaching, and it would have been unwise to proceed further that day. On the summit of the hill first taken the Arawas now collected and began to discuss the situation. It was evidently a foregone conclusion. They were resolved to do no more. Many excuses were made. We should soon be short of powder. We had no food. Let us send back for a convoy for supplies. I agreed to send back, but this concession was of no use. They went on speaking all the evening, Major Roberts holding the hill with the A. C. in an untouched position meanwhile.

At last the natives returned to camp, and Fox brought me the ultimatum of his tribe. They wished to return, and in point of fact, I knew, meant to go back if I refused my consent. The question of sending for further supplies settled itself, as no native bearers could be induced to undertake the service.

Fox, however, was by no means proud of the conduct of the Arawa, and assured me that if I went to Waikare he would go with me, and thought that if I called for volunteers many of his friends would share our fortunes. I accordingly tried this experiment and sixty Arawas volunteered. To have pushed on to Waikare without some natives would have been foolhardy, as their experience of the bush and knowledge of rough expedients would have been indispensable to us in crossing an arm of the lake, which I was led to believe I must in some way pass to reach the enemy's *pah*.

The Arawas and other natives now wrote me a letter bearing out Fox's report of their resolution to return, and I discovered that there had throughout been an understanding among them not to go beyond Ruatahuna. This had been kept secret from me, and that, too, although it had been carefully explained beforehand that they were required to go to Waikare and Maungapowhaki. An officer in this warfare often finds his plans thwarted and the safety of his force endangered by such strikes among the native allies. On this occasion the result was not disastrous, but it might easily have been so. We had accomplished the main object of the expedition, and as it subsequently proved Colonel Herrick had not started on his march towards us, no great inconvenience arose from the conduct of the Arawa on this occasion. But had the third column been in difficulties the case might have been very different.

As it was, I still felt bound to try to collect a column for the service, and consequently arranged to divide the force, sending back the wounded with those who would not go any further by the Horomanga gorge, and remaining between them and the Waikare gorge till I could determine whether it was prudent to push on to the lake with the remaining force. I divided the reserve ammunition equally between the two columns, and crossed the Whakatane to another camping ground with the column intended for Waikare. During the night, however, Fox's followers came to a decision neither to accompany the wounded nor go on with me to the lake, but to go home.

Fox in reporting this told me he had tried but could not alter their determination. The Europeans upon whom the hardships of the expedition told far more than on the Maoris, whose boots were worn out by the incessant crossing of rivers with sharp shale bottoms, and who were not accustomed to a potato diet, nevertheless showed a spirit and cheerfulness beyond all praise. They were willing and ready to march to the possible assistance of their comrades of the third column, at all events towards the enemy at Waikare, and they were not discouraged by the knowledge that with their bleeding feet and insufficient food they must march and camp two days in the snow of the Huirau range.

But I had to consider the risk, the small chance of success without the co-operation of at least some Maoris, in traversing so long a forest path and crossing one branch of the lake, and I had to bear in mind the necessary abandonment of our present line when once the position of Ruatahuna was evacuated, and that anything less than complete success and the capture of a settlement well provided with food at the end of our march would cause a disaster the extent of which could hardly be estimated.

In such operations, while all fair risks must be run, a very small error, a very trifling want of judgment might produce terrible results, and on the whole I preferred to risk the possibility of not being at hand to aid Colonel Herrick to that of sacrificing the whole force I had at my disposal at Ruatahuna. At all events Colonel Herrick had failed me, and the expedition could not be kept longer in the mountains. If prevented advancing by the enemy it was probable that Colonel Herrick had long ago retired to a place of safety. If he had not yet started, he could hardly expect to find me at Ruatahuna so long after the date of rendezvous.

In this dilemma I chose the course I believed best for the colony, however humiliating it might be to be thus dictated to by our allies. On the 14th we commenced the return march to Ahikereru, which we reached without molestation on the 16th. Here we found supplies awaiting us, and on the following day we returned to Fort Galatea, being joined late in the evening by Major Mair and the native column, which like ourselves had experienced no serious opposition on the march.

Marching myself with Colonel Roberts' column homewards, by a parallel line and nearer to the enemy's force, I still had felt great anxiety for the safety of the column under Major Mair. Because I felt convinced that a determined attack of the enemy might at any moment produce a stampede, in which the cry of "*sauve qui peut*" would drown the remonstrances of those who wished to defend the helpless sufferers in their charge. But happily, the discomfiture of the Uriweras had been too complete, and the demoralisation of the tribe too pronounced to admit of any serious effort for the time. Major Mair had had sufficient difficulty to keep his force from hurrying on without regard to the progress of the wounded, to show what a few well-directed shots would have done in the way of disorganising his column, but his firm and judicious management of the natives had its effect, and the column reached Fort Galatea in good order.

The natives were inordinately proud of their achievement, and of having resisted the temptation to hurry on and leave the rear to take care of itself. In fact, Petera Pukuatua made no small boast of his hero-ism and devotion in delaying for the wounded he had in charge, and afforded an excellent example of the sort of support a colonial com-mander may expect from friendly natives should he unfortunately be driven to rely upon their assistance in moments of real danger.

Such was the Uriwera expedition, undertaken with the double object of punishing the mountain tribe and of destroying the stores of provisions without which, at all events, Te Kooti's followers, who were not accustomed to the rough bush food that sufficed for the hardier Uriweras, could not remain in the locality. The success had been com-plete; not only had the enemy lost a considerable number of his men, but he had measured his strength five or six times with us, in positions carefully chosen, and found it impossible either to repulse or even to inflict serious loss upon our columns.

On no occasion had he gained any material success, but on the contrary had always found himself resolutely attacked in his ambus-cade and driven off at once. The difficulties of the march and of the supply of the men had been got over satisfactorily, and the Uriwera had learned that neither were sufficient to protect them in future as they had proved in the past.

The adjacent tribes who had for centuries regarded the strongholds of the Uriwera as being not only difficult to assail but, for practical purposes, impregnable, were disillusioned by our success. The supersti-tions of the past being dissipated, the result in the early future was seen in the native expeditions of Ropata and Kemp, who for the first time on record entered the mountains unhesitatingly when ordered to do so a year later by Mr. McLean. Our men had given proof in their con-duct during the expedition of the great superiority of our race when placed upon terms of equality with the native one.

An ordinary English soldier, trained to fight in the open, will march determinedly to attack a battery belching forth volleys of iron hail; but the same man thrown into a jungle, called upon to fight invisible savages, has too often shown to disadvantage. The reason is evident. A brave dragoon might well quail to furl a sail in the breeze—he is out of his element, unaccustomed to the position, or even to thinking of finding himself so situated. Our men had by this time got over the difficulty which oppressed them at first.

Six months' continuous marching and fighting in the bush had destroyed its terrors, and they were now able to do anything except to run as fast as their naked native opponents, and as regards their pluck, constancy, discipline, and use of their arms, they were better beyond comparison.

CHAPTER 11

End of the War, and General Reflections

The exposure and fatigue had told upon me, and I was now compelled to leave the field, suffering from acute dysentery, from which I had scarcely recovered before I found myself crippled with rheumatism. I was obliged therefore to resign the active command in the field to Lieut.-Colonel St. John, and, after obtaining medical advice at Auckland, proceeded to Wellington to assist the government by such advice and information as I was able to afford. But I left stringent orders with the force to advance the main camp to Opepe or Taupo for reasons based upon the calculations made before the campaign began, and upon the assumption that all our objects having been obtained, Te Kooti must in a very few weeks break cover and come out on the plains.

The third column had not moved. Mr. Richmond, thinking that the best if not the only way to reach the enemy's position was by water, had directed boats and pontoon rafts to be constructed, which at that distance inland, and without appliances save such as could with difficulty be brought up, proved a task requiring far more time than he had anticipated.

The consequence was that this expensive expedition, which did not eventually aid towards the general object of the campaign, became simply a demonstration against the enemy's *pah* on the opposite shore. Nay more, having commenced the undertaking, there was a not unnatural disinclination to withdraw and seem to acknowledge failure, without at all events crossing the lake and capturing the Waikare *pah*. We had been therefore weakened by the absence of the force without gaining any adequate advantage, while we had been very near attempting a dangerous, painful, and difficult operation to support loyally a column which could not have succeeded for a month later at least.

The mistake was one which shows how essential it is in war that there should be no division of command, at least in the same operations. If Lieut.-Colonel Herrick had been directed simply to reach Ruatahuna on a certain day, and told if the lake could not be crossed in time to march round its shore, he would have come up as intended. To have marched round it was quite feasible, and indeed was afterwards accomplished by Mr. Hamlin and a native party.

I am certain that Colonel Herrick had he received such orders would have allowed nothing to prevent his carrying them out, and in all human probability he would have reached the rendezvous successfully. As it was, a fine force was locked up and unable to co-operate, and the long bill so incurred was made the most of in Parliament as a weapon of attack upon the government. Yet it had been the result of a generous effort of the Native Minister to lighten my work. All, however, proved to have been fulfilled.

Te Kooti found before long that the food for his following no longer existed, and as signs that he was outstaying his welcome began to be manifested, he very soon left the Uriweras and marched for Taupo with his own band and a few volunteers from the mountain tribe. Before leaving the force I gave positive orders to Lieut.-Colonel St. John to take the earliest possible opportunity of moving the head-quarter camp forwards from Fort Galatea to a suitable point on the road from the Uriwera Mountains to Taupo, and indicated Opepe, the point where the Napier road crossed the main track from Taupo to the Rangitaiki Valley, as the best strategical position, if otherwise suitable.

Failing Opepe, either Tapuaikereru the northern point of the lake or some intermediate spot was to be selected; but as Opepe afforded both wood and water as well as better grass than usually found on the plains I thought if possible, it should be occupied. I had collected with immense trouble a large supply of biscuit and other stores as well as of ammunition at Fort Galatea, and when the main camp was established on the Napier road, I calculated upon a second line of supply from another and better base.

From various causes, however, it was not till June 6th that Colonel St. John felt able to take preliminary steps to carry out his orders, and on that day, he proceeded to examine the site of Opepe with a cavalry escort. Captain St. George in command at Tapuaeharuru joined him, and by the 7th, having satisfactorily fixed a camping ground, Lieut.-Colonel St. John was induced to direct his escort to halt at Opepe while he himself rode over to Captain St. George's quarters at Tap-uaeharuru. Up to this time everything had been quiet in the district, and the probable approach of Te Kooti, upon which I had reckoned with certainty, seems to have been entirely overlooked by Captain St. George and his natives. Lieut.-Colonel St. John, rendered too confi-dent by their assurances, told his men that they need apprehend no danger, that a sentry was unnecessary, and that they might rest and feed their horses till his return next day.

Two gentlemen returning to Napier from Tapuaeharuru, on the morning of the 8th, came upon two dead bodies lying stripped on the highway near Opepe. They turned back and made their report to Lieut.-Colonel St. John whom they met coming back to his escort, with Captain St. George. Lieut.-Colonel St. John at once sent back Captain St. George to collect some friendly natives, and after wait-ing till nightfall again moved on himself when they came up, so as to reach Opepe by daybreak. At Opepe nine dead bodies were found and traces of a considerable native force which had passed on southwards.

This lamentable surprise, the direct consequence of the unfortu-nate delay in obeying my orders, and of over-confidence, did much to retrieve Te Kooti's prestige. He had left the mountains with only the following of 100 men, and on reaching Opepe had conversed with some of the escort, pretending that the force was a friendly con-tingent. When the whole of his men arrived, the unfortunate escort was attacked unexpectedly while unarmed, and all those that could be reached were shot. One or two, including the cornet in com-mand, made their escape and reached Galatea, spreading unnecessarily gloomy reports and discouraging the men already suffering from the cold, tedium, and hardship of their life on the plains.

Lieut.-Colonel St. John had hitherto kept them employed in road-making to facilitate the transport of supplies, but to do so he had to subsist them from the reserve provisions brought up with so much difficulty by pack horses to Galatea. It had been a strong additional reason for an early movement to Opepe that by that means the supply at Fort Galatea would not be exhausted, as Napier could have been relied upon to furnish ample provisions and meat, the latter being most difficult to obtain at Galatea.

Thus, a reserve depot would always have been accessible in case of stoppage on the Napier line, and I had intended to have collected a large supply from both directions at Opepe. To eke out the Galatea supplies the ration was not increased as the extreme cold required, nor would it have been necessary to economize at all had the camp been pushed on say by May 20th or 24th. After the reverse at Opepe, not in itself important, it was unfortunate that Lieut.-Colonel St. John did not at once collect every available man, and move by forced marches over the doubtful tribes whom he could easily overawe if they saw no chance of our protection.

But it was otherwise ordered, and Te Kooti's prestige enormously increased by an apparent unwillingness to try conclusions with him, even with an immensely superior force and in the open plains. By doing this we seemed to accept the unfortunate surprise of a small escort as an overwhelming defeat to our arms, compelling a complete evacuation of an enormous breadth of territory and once more leaving the road open to Te Kooti to resume his razzias upon the peaceful settlements of the coast.

Beginning this when a very few weeks must have ended the war, in a manner and at a spot which would have taught its own lesson to the sulky Kingites not far off, it is not wonderful that government found the hostilities so nearly concluded when they took office still continuing in a guerilla form a year later; and when it is remembered that by a more vigorous course we had in the preceding seven months, created a force, retrieved our disasters, re-conquered our lost districts, and defeated the enemy on the West Coast who had been more or less in arms for nine years, besides conducting a campaign on the East Coast so nearly to an equally satisfactory conclusion that we had reduced assistance to the small focus of 100 men on the Taupo plains, it is easy to compare the advantages reaped by the colony from one system and the other.

Mr. Fox's government had a trained, proved and reliable force to hand. Unlike its predecessors, it was not obliged to conduct war with men always months in arrears of pay; for they paid the troops out of loans. It had, too, only one side of the island to think about, and on that the enemy was not occupying a dense and pathless bush, nor in numbers to cause the smallest anxiety. Yet the war, so nearly ended when Mr. Fox took office in 1869, more than a year later, continued in a desultory way, and fourteen months elapsed before Te Kooti was at last suffered to go back with his followers almost unpursued and unmolested, to the safe asylum of the Uriwera country.

Meanwhile he had been slowly hunted round Lake Taupo till at last with his force, when the crops of the Uriwera were again ripe, he was able to regain the shelter of the mountains from which so much pains had been taken to dislodge him. How all this occurred I am not the person to explain. This should be done by the officer whom the government affected to trust with the command, but treated with neither confidence nor support from the first, and finally made the scapegoat of its own shortcomings.

Possibly Colonel McDonnell may have erred sometimes, but the Duke of Wellington must have failed had he been tied hand and foot as he was. The regular or A. C. force Colonel McDonnell did not then belong to, though he commanded such men and officers as happened to be serving with him. It had been the earnest endeavour of the late government and of all the officers of the A. C. to implant a military spirit into the only approach to a regular force which we possessed. To a very great extent they had succeeded in this, though as the late Major von Tempsky said, where a force has no history and no traditions it is not easy to create an *esprit de corps.*

The virulent and unmerited abuse political windbags showered upon the character of the A. C., however successful in rendering the force unpopular in the country, united the men in a fellow-feeling of injustice that all experienced. By fostering the military spirit which was undoubtedly growing fast in the force, the government might have achieved almost anything with the men that British pluck, devotion, and endurance could accomplish.

But the new government, at the outset, decided upon taking a step as unwise as it was distasteful to the force, and in one day destroyed the military character of the constabulary. Mr. Brannigan, a Police Commissioner from Otago, who enjoyed the character of being very smart in that capacity, but who had no experience in commanding military bodies, was appointed to the command of the force. His first step was to break up the divisions which had each their own individuality in our little history, which created an emulation in each to be smarter than the rest. Policemen's rattles were issued to men who hitherto had only used the rifle. The uniform was to be at once modified to the police pattern. And a code of bye-laws was drawn up for the government of the force, very suitable for a city police, but hardly for troops in the field; while a multitude of reports and returns were ordered to be sent in with the utmost punctuality, which in themselves would have taken up half of every officer's time to prepare.

These initiatory steps disgusted both officers and men, and destroyed their self-respect. It was not only that they had been placed under the command of an officer who was a pure civilian, but that it was quite clear that they were now policemen, not soldiers. The new regime was inaugurated by many propitiatory sacrifices, and the best and bravest men felt that they were specially selected for the prescribed list. Many, unable to bear the humiliation of the new system and disgusted at the espionage, encouraged and even directed by the government, resigned their appointments. Others, excellent men in every respect, were turned out of the force pitilessly without notice, and in fact a reign of terror began in which the character and utility of the force, as a military protection to the country, was entirely destroyed.

Colonel McDonnell had therefore but a small mainstay to rely upon as the backbone of the heterogeneous assemblages he was called upon to command. Moreover, he had to put up with the jealousy of the new Commissioner, who resented the employment of his men in the field under another. It really looked as if the government wished to rule the military forces in the field on the Austrian principle of *divide et impera.* How many commanders there were, all more or less independent and yet each directing portions of the force employed during the same operations, it is hard to say. Their name was legion.

For instance, there was Mr. Brannigan in Waikato burning to do something to gain the confidence of the force by his conduct in the field. There was Colonel Moule also in Waikato controlling the militia and volunteers, while the "Carnot" of the War Department, Mr. McLean, controlled both from the other end of the telegraph wire in Auckland. Then there was Colonel Fraser at Tauranga with the bulk of the A. C. strictly obeying his orders by displaying a masterly inactivity, yet whose force in two or three marches might have enabled Colonel McDonnell, who was the only one doing any work and should have been supreme, to bring Te Kooti to decisive action at any time.

Then there were the chiefs Kemp and Topia, with the Wanganuis, Colonel Herrick, and later, Major Roberts, all only partially under Colonel McDonnell; and lastly, the most important of all, the Commissariat Department administered independently from Napier by Mr. Ormond, on purely economical principles, and cutting things so close that Colonel McDonnell rarely had a complete day's ration at all, never knew when to expect a convoy, and was always absolutely without a reserve. It might have been foreseen that either Colonel McDonnell should have been left unfettered and absolutely supreme over all detachments and departments, or he should have been removed, and an officer to whom the government was willing to confide such powers appointed in his place. Half trust and perpetual interference could have but one result, failure and delay.

Some three months after the general retreat to the coast, every position, then so wantonly abandoned, had to be reoccupied. Te Kooti from being a fugitive with but 100 men had regained all his prestige, was at the head of a considerable force, and actually had made a triumphal progress through the Maori king's country. He had entered into relations with Rewi and other kingite chiefs, and had he met with any remarkable success, they would undoubtedly have taken up arms on his side, and a war to last for years might have ensued. Parliament being prorogued the Ministry was able to act as it pleased, and, alarmed at the dangerous results of the retreat policy, it was resolved to assemble a force once more in the interior.

Accordingly, from north, south, east, and west, detachments on no particular plan were hurried towards Lake Taupo, affording Te Kooti an opportunity of attacking them in detail, of which he took advantage. Having struck one or two blows, however, Colonel McDonnell, who had come up, assembled some of the detachments, and drove him back at Pourere beyond Rotorua. At length opportunity occurred to strike a decisive blow. Te Kooti entrenched himself with his force at Poutou, south of Taupo some twelve miles, and was attacked and defeated by Colonel McDonnell. The action I shall not describe as I was not present, but it was a success which, had it been followed up, would have ended the war. But there were no provisions for a pursuit, as the government preferred economising the supplies and leaving the men to waste their energies and time in searching for potatoes. Thus, the force had, after a movement in advance, to retire to dig its dinner.

As the line of supply passed through perfectly safe, easy and open country, this commissariat economy, to most minds, was inexplicable. It was, however, appreciated by Te Kooti, who speedily took heart after his defeat and retired upon the king's country. Meanwhile, Mr. Fox had sent a native contingent, under Topia, up the Wanganui River to Taupo, for what purpose nobody could understand. Half the cost so incurred applied in the supply of portable rations to Colonel McDonnell would have left nothing more to be done. Te Kooti was, however, safe for a while, the government having issued the most stringent orders to prevent Colonel McDonnell pursuing him across the king's boundary.

After a while Mr. McLean attempted personal negotiation with Rewi, and was received in a peculiarly humiliating manner by that chief and others. The nearest to a practical proposition got out of them was a suggestion by Rewi that we should lay down our arms first, and then, perhaps, Te Kooti would lay down his. To such a point had our imbecile management of affairs made us contemptible in the eyes of the warlike Waikatos, who a few short months before had been waiting day by day to hear that Te Kooti and his few adherents had been utterly destroyed at Taupo.

Though the Kingites would neither arrest nor attack Te Kooti to please Mr. McLean, they still did not wish to have their district compromised, perhaps invaded, in consequence of his presence, so as soon as the Minister left, they politely requested the rebel leader to "move on." Refreshed and recruited, Te Kooti obligingly took his departure and repaired to the Patetere country, where the people favoured him and his "religion."

Here Colonel McDonnell, had he been a free agent, would probably again have signally defeated the enemy. But circumstanced as he was it was hopeless.

Fifteen or sixteen hundred men were all near, but none except Colonel McDonnell's own column came up. All waited the signal, not from their commander, but from the War Minister, who failed to give it till the chance was lost. The Waikato force stood still. Te Kooti burst through Colonel McDonnell's force by a surprise and got clear away. Marching on, he met and defeated Colonel Fraser, slowly coming up by the bush, and drove him back to Tauranga. Last of all he made for Rotorua, and if he could have surprised that place his path was open to the mountains across the only practicable ford of the Rangitaiki, carefully left unguarded, at Fort Galatea. He did not, however, succeed in carrying out his programme quite as successfully as he had expected, for a French-Canadian half-breed, named Baker, a deserter from one of H. M. ships of war, who had long resided among the Maoris, brought the intelligence of his design to Captain Gilbert Mair at Ohinemuri.

Thereupon, hurriedly assembling a scratch force, Captain Gilbert Mair moved out and attacked Te Kooti, who made off towards Fort Galatea. But Captain Mair, who for his gallantry afterwards received, on my recommendation, the New Zealand Cross, held Te Kooti's rear-guard in a continual skirmish at very close quarters, killing some eighteen or twenty of his best men, and only giving up the pursuit at nightfall. This feat of arms accomplished by a few irregulars, almost all Maoris, was one of the most brilliant episodes of the war, and but for the miserable mistake of leaving Fort Galatea unoccupied might have, even then, enabled the colony to extricate itself with some credit from the struggle. It is worth remarking that the stable was carefully locked afterwards when the steed was gone, and Galatea was garrisoned for the future, though perhaps never to be of any use again.

Thus, ended these operations which, after fourteen months, left us in a worse position than ever. Somebody had to bear the blame. Some scapegoat had to be found; Colonel Fraser happened to die just then, Mr. Brannigan and Colonel Moule had not been suffered to lift their fingers by their imperious master. Mr. Ormond was too influential a member of the party, and Mr. McLean too necessary to it, to be called to account; there remained only poor Colonel McDonnell, more sinned against than sinning, who had really not been responsible for any part of the failure, but had been grossly ill-used in being so much interfered with. So, Colonel McDonnell was recalled, and the command suffered to devolve or revolve between Ropata and Kemp (English troops not being competent, in the opinion of Ministers, to do the work).

Happily, the expedition of 1869 had burst the bubble of superstition which till then had protected the Uriwera, and Kemp and Ropata penetrated and hunted the mountains from hill to hill, almost unresisted. Two successes occurred, one of which might have had very important results. It had been the outcome of operations designed and carried out by Kemp, but owing to the jealousies or want of concert between the rival leaders, the attack was made by Ropata too soon, while Kemp was endeavouring to surround the position, and thus the enemy escaped. After this no further active operations on a large scale were attempted. Small expeditions of enlisted Maoris under Mair, Preece, Porter, and Hamlin, traversed the mountains in all directions, practically unopposed, seeking for Te Kooti.

After evading their pursuit for several months, the New Zealand Nana Sahib at length gathered some of his followers and was suffered to depart openly enough, but unpursued, and sought refuge in the king's country. There, having but a remnant of his old following, he remained quiet and unmolested till, some years later, the Hon. Mr. Bryce, then Native Minister, invited the outlaw, as he was still regarded, to meet him at the king's settlement, Whatiwhatihoe, under the Pirongia ranges, in the Upper Waikato.

On this occasion Mr. Bryce shook hands with Te Kooti and extended to him the amnesty from which he had hitherto been specially excluded. Following upon this, not only was the proclamation, offering £5000 for his head, formally revoked, but, with the magnanimity so characteristic of the British nation, coupled with this pardon was the gift of a house and section of land at Kihikihi, which the government had purchased for that purpose. Here Te Kooti peacefully ended his remarkable career, living for several years on terms of amity with his neighbours and dying at length "in the odour of sanctity."

Te Kooti's public submission was, in point of fact, the final act in the Maori war which had disturbed the colony for so many years and had cost, from first to last, some millions of money.

I have endeavoured in these pages to tell an unvarnished, truthful story of how the Self-Reliant policy was put in force by the Colonial Government, and the Maoris made to feel, once for all, that the struggle against British supremacy was a useless one. There is no reason to apprehend any future disturbances. The whites and the Maoris are now practically one people, and the best feeling exists between the two races. It finds its parallel in the relations subsisting between the English and French Canadians in the great Dominion. Firmness tempered by kindness is the true policy of the future.

In short, to use the words of the brave old Sir Harry Smith, the hero of Aliwal, let us teach the Maoris by our policy towards them that while "we have a heart for peace, we have an arm for war."(The Hero of Aliwal by James Humphries is also published by Leonaur.)

A Sketch of the New Zealand War

Faithfully yours
Morgan S Grace

Contents

To

V.C. SIR ANTHONY HOME K.C.B

AN EMINENTLY DISTINGUISHED MAN, WHOSE LITERARY TASTE IS
ONLY

SURPASSED BY HIS PERSONAL COURAGE, THIS BRIEF SKETCH IS

DEDICATED. MY ADMIRATION FOR HIS PURE LOVE OF

JUSTICE AND TRUTH SUGGESTED THIS NARRATIVE,

AND THE PLEASURE I TAKE IN CONTEMPLATING

HIS SURPRISE AT ITS DETAILS

GIVES ZEST TO THIS EFFORT TO

RENEW MY YOUTH.

Preface

This sketch of the Maori War is not intended to have any merit except spontaneity. I have consulted no authorities, read no despatches.

I hold that no one who was a participator in the events of this war could realise its true character by reading the published accounts of it.

I have a photographic plate in my brain of everything that I saw, from which I can strike off pictures at will. And I can act as a phonograph of everything I heard. I can describe and narrate by word of mouth without difficulty, but I am a cramped writer, and mere penmanship makes my progress like that of a horse galloping with his legs tied. All the same, as I shall soon be dead and gone, I now give effect to the wish I have had in my mind for more than thirty years.

I scorn a lie in any form, not merely on account of its intrinsic faultiness (for I have known dozens of fine fellows in all walks of life lie on occasion without circumstance), but because, if I told a lie, I would have to own up at once and take the consequences, lest my adversary should think I was afraid of him. What I have written I have seen or heard from true and worthy witnesses, and if you will look through my eyes, you will see it also. The knowledge cannot fail of a humanizing effect. You will thus learn what blundering asses we were, and what fine fellows the Maoris.

Introduction

The experiences of the Anglo-Saxon race in its relations with the Maoris have always been uncommon. The Maoris from the commencement practically asserted his superiority, and in many essentials has justified the assertion.

It will be remembered that in the early trading days a Maori chief always spoke of a White Man as his *Pakeha* (White Man). The trader's privileges were based on the Maori chiefs' proprietary claims. The White Man had no inherent rights. His life and property were really at the mercy of the chief. The Maoris, being essentially a gentleman, wrapped this thorn deftly in rose leaves. Its existence, however, was real.

It is a fact, that Bishop Pompalier, on first landing north of Auckland, presented himself in full canonicals, mitre on head and pastoral staff in hand. The Maoris surrounded him, flourishing their tomahawks, and deliberately undressed him to examine into the character of his pretensions. When they came to his undershirt and drawers, His Grace the Archbishop made signs to them that good manners dictated restraint of their curiosity. They respected his wishes, but tried on all his garments. As he had exhibited much amiability and dignified sweetness, they assisted him to re-robe, and led him to their *runanga*-house, treating him with every consideration.

The attitude of the chiefs to the Church of England missioners was characterised by the dignified respect due from great functionaries to each other. The Maoris showed themselves above prejudice. This was clearly displayed in a theological discussion conducted in the Auckland district by the Maoris adherents of the Catholic and Anglican Churches as to the Church of England claim of Apostolical succession and consequent authority.

A great meeting was assembled in Waikato. The Maoris devoted ten days to the public discussion, which was held in the open air. The astute Catholic advocate yielded the honour of opening the debate to the Anglican, as New Zealand was a British Colony. He then took two and a half summer days to reply. He had by him a bundle of sticks. He planted the first in the ground, christening it St. Peter, and gave a sketch of St. Peter's life and works. He followed this up by placing a labelled stick for each of the Popes in historical succession, sketching each worthy's story, and, when he came to the period of the Reformation, pointed with emphasis to the break in the Anglican line. The Maoris, who cared only for the argument, gave the decision by acclamation in favour of the Catholic Church.

The debate was an admirable instance of the faculty of sustained attention to discussion shown by the Maoris in listening; of the power of order and concentration shown by their orators, with the force of conviction at the root of the effort; and of the acuteness of the Maoris, already as great in theology as his teacher. The same capacity to excel is seen today in the Maoris within the walls of Parliament. He is unsurpassed either as a political strategist in party warfare, in eloquence if words avail, or in reticence if mystery is likely to forward his objects. The result is, he often holds the balance of power between political parties, and whilst loudly declaiming that the rights of his race are always made subservient to the interests of the white people, has really for a quarter of a century escaped the payment of his legitimate portion of the land-tax, whilst benefiting enormously by the construction of railways, macadamised roads, and expensive bridges leading to his landed property at the cost of the colony.

So well has the Maoris managed editors and public opinion generally that it has been customary to say the Maori has been robbed of his land by the European. I have no hesitation whatever in affirming that the European has been robbed of his money by the Maoris, under the sanction of the most approved, gentlemanly, courteous methods.

It must not be forgotten that the Maori's title to his lands was attained by conquest and occupation. There was no constitutional law to guide the Maoris. He occupied by force, and defended his occupation by war. Whatever the aggressions of the Anglo-Saxons, their power to make treaties was always regulated by the constitutional law obtaining in the British Isles. A reference to *The Law of Nations* (Ed. 1834), by Chitty; to the Charter of Lord Carlisle; to Sir Humphrey Gilbert's Charter for Virginia; and to the Letters Patent to John Cabot, proves that England had no legal sanction to make a treaty bearing the interpretation which the pressure of the Church Missionary Society and Exeter Hall subsequently gave to the Treaty of Waitangi. The true meaning of the Treaty of Waitangi as understood by the Maoris and interpreted by Anglo-Saxon law and usage was that the Maoris were protected in possession of all the lands they had hunted over or cultivated. In the end the Europeans were cheated into buying from the Maoris millions of acres of land which the native New Zealander had never seen.

So much for the statecraft of the Maoris. The missioner interpreted the Treaty of Waitangi for him: the Maori took the profit and repudiated his benefactor. In dealings for land with private individuals it is true that the Maoris sometimes had the worst of the bargain, but quite as frequently the European found that when he had paid for the land the Maori seller subsidized other claimants to upset the title, and remained in the enjoyment of his tribal claim to the property after he had spent the price obtained for it in feasting his relations. It was from the beginning a case of diamond cut diamond, and as nothing could really impoverish the Maori as long as there remained to him the tribal right to live on and with his own people, the chocolate-brown diamond cut the deepest. So much for the Maoris in peace. I hope presently to delineate some of his warlike characteristics.

CHAPTER 1

My Early Days

I was the delicate son of a highly intellectual mother: physically the poorest specimen of a large family. I adored my mother with the reverence which a feeble child feels for a protector. She never showed a particle of partiality for me. Indeed, mothers rarely set their hearts on any but their eldest or youngest children, and her eldest son was stormily successful from the cradle up. He conquered all difficulties with the air of an emperor, and kicked or cuffed or bluffed his way up to the top of any circle in which he moved. He was a fine fellow: I was not.

I had, however, enough of a child's subtlety to enable me on most occasions to find ingenious excuses for the difficult positions into which I drifted.

In course of time my health became so weak it was thought desirable to send me to a farm in the country, called Sheadogue, which was owned by my father, and managed by what in Scotland is called a bailiff. Here I acquired that attachment to the people which has since given me the freedom of their hearts. I went to school with a lot of bare-footed, ragged-breeched urchins, who first instilled heroism into my soul. Their theory was "blood is blood." They showed me ruined abbeys, broken-down bridges, tumbling walls, Gothic tombs and chapels; all of which, I was assured, belonged to my ancestors. This was a revelation. My mother's mind was ascetic: my maternal grandmother was a Scotch Calvinist. All this field had been hidden from me, and now, with the acute perception of a child's mind, I saw trouble in store.

I could not feel that I had "any blood" in me, and yet I knew that argument was out of the question. As I foresaw, when any difficulty arose to bar our boyish objects, everyone exclaimed, "Blood is blood," and I was called to the front

Nobody could have been more unfit for the position. It was useless to reason, so I did my best. Sometimes I had to engage in personal conflict a champion from some other barony. The result was invariably disastrous. On these occasions my backers used to lift me off the ground, and wipe the blood off my face with my cap, saying, "You are powerful weak entirely. Never mind, 'blood is blood.' Go in again." And I did, with the same result, until a general scrimmage resulted, at which I was better, as, though very slight and small, I was as active as a squirrel, and knew how to hearten others.

These experiences accustomed my mind to tribal disputes and irregular warfare, and I make these disclosures to warn the reader that my sympathies are with the Maoris, though my affections are all with the British soldier, who in adversity or success is a child of nature.

Chapter 2

Arrival in Auckland

I arrived in Auckland in June,1860, in medical charge of troops.We had touched at Sydney and heard of the Maoris War. Communication was scant at that time, and but little was known. Enough, however, to make me feel the Maori tomahawk crunch through my skull into the brain.

Nothing can be more charming than the first view of Auckland. I have seen many beautiful cities in Europe, Asia, America, and Australia. I doubt whether any compare favourably with Auckland in situation and surroundings. It looked to us weary voyagers a haven of rest. No one could believe that in such a lovely country, so peaceful, so attractive, war could be possible.

The troops on landing were met by a military band, and marched up Queen Street, surrounded by a rejoicing people.We brought fresh hope and joy to anxious colonists.The affair at Waireka had left a poor impression as to the efficacy of British troops in Maori warfare, and anxiety and alarm pervaded the public mind.

I reported myself to the chief medical officer, and left a card on the *commandant's* daughter. How well do I remember her first question— "Well, what do you think of Auckland?"

I stood up, looked out of the window, and said, "Beautiful! It is a thousand pities, however, the North Shore is not planted."

I turned round, looked at the circle in the drawing-room, and said to myself, "These people think me a prig. I wonder why?"

I was detailed for duty at the General Hospital in Auckland City, and settled down to my work. In a few days a very nice, gentlemanly man—a brother medical officer—said to me, "I have my orders for the seat of war.Your arrival has played the devil with everything. I am making love to the sweetest gal in the world. Long before my return (if I ever return) some combatant officer will have carried her off."

I felt the cold shivers run down my back, and the whistle of the Maori bullet in my ear. I muttered to myself, "Blood is blood," and said to him:—

My dear fellow, I am dying to go to the seat of war. I am a poor devil of an Irishman, accustomed to a turbulent people. I have seen the lady: she is a beauty. For her sweet sake, I'll be off and get tomahawked. I will volunteer for active service. You have friends: you can manage the rest.

And he did.

CHAPTER 3

Off to the War

I was ordered to the seat of war, and paraded with the rest in the barrack square preparatory to the march to Onehunga. I had on my undress staff frock-coat; I have it still. It would not go within six inches of buttoning round my waist now.

The men of the 65th who paraded were shaggy, bearded giants, roughly clad, with their arms in excellent order. In comparison, I looked a dandy, and knew it. I had served recently with the Rifles. The brigade-major, mounted on a rough ten-pound animal, rode straight at me, pulled his horse on his haunches, swung him a bit to the left, and shouted out:—

You think yourself a swell, sir. I am Brigade-Major Slack. You are going to Taranaki. Tell Colonel Gold, sir, he is bitching the whole war. As for Colonel Murray, I shall have him broke, sir, I shall have him broke. I have reported the whole business to the Horse Guards.

He rode off. I smiled, and ranked him a shingle short. We embarked in the ss. *Airedale*. She was so uncommonly low in the water and so crowded with men that I felt sure she would topple over. With every roll of the boat the soldiers on deck felt their left or their right. The weather fortunately was fine. We arrived off New Plymouth early in the morning, and landed in surf-boats. I was met on the beach by a cheerful-looking young officer with 65 on his forage cap, who said, "You had better go up to the mess-room, and have some breakfast"

I inquired my way, and was directed to a long, two-storeyed shed; walked upstairs, and entered a bare wooden room with a long trestle table in it. It was apparently empty. A corner was cut off by a rough paper screen.

I walked up to a shabby mirror over the mantelpiece, arranged my hair, and settled my silk stock. I had landed in my undress frock-coat—in fact I had never had it off since I left Auckland—and felt very uncomfortable. A stage-whisper broke on the silence of the room:—

Begorra, Mick, here is another of them patent-leather French soldiers, just like Captain Richards of the Light Bobs.

To explain this, it is necessary to say that a blue frock-coat is not a regimental uniform,

I was a staff-assistant surgeon, and therefore had no regimental uniform.

I glanced through a chink in the screen, and saw a pair of honest grey eyes contemplating me with scorn. Without turning round, and whilst still arranging my hair, I called for stirabout and milk. There was a smothered guffaw behind the screen. A fine, handsome soldier walked out, and said:—

"Begorra, sir, there is no stirabout and milk in this country at all, at all; but I can order for you rashers and eggs."

"Rashers and eggs by all means let it be."

We were both quite grave, but each had in his eye an amused twinkle that was more eloquent than words. This incident got about amongst the soldiers, and made me free of the 65th Foot.

CHAPTER 4

Soldier's Account of the War

Next day I put away my undress frockcoat, and wore a blue jumper and a forage cap to show my rank. I now give you a soldier's account of the war up to the date of my arrival:—

"This was a bit of a ruction about land. Outsiders had nothing to do with it. We could have managed it all ourselves, but we were not going to be hurried. After we had time to get warm there would have been some fine fighting. Then we would have settled our quarrels, had a big feed together, and gone on again, in a comfortable, easy manner. You see, the 65th has been in New Zealand about eighteen years. We all talk the language, more or less. Indeed, some of us have close relations amongst the Maoris. Whether or not, they are a decent, civil-spoken race, and we know many of their chiefs and people as well as we do our messmates.

"Well, Wiremu Kingi insulted Governor Gore Brown by saying, 'The Waitara is mine. I will not allow its sale.' When requested to talk the matter over with the Governor, Wiremu said—

"'It is for me to talk, for others to keep silent.'

"He then left the meeting in a dudgeon, and walked off with his followers.

"Governor Gore Brown considered the queen in his person insulted, and ordered the survey of the land and the completion of the purchase from Te Teira, who was friendly to the *Pakeha*, and a great ruffian. Wiremu Kingi built a *pa* on the disputed block, and we were sent out to storm the *pa*. All this was in perfect good blood. Wiremu Kingi knew we were going to attack, and some of his men marched with us when we were on the way to surprise it.

"The *pa* was not a fighting stockade; it was what the Maoris call

171

WIREMU KINGI

a 'land title *pa*.' Wiremu had defended his title by the erection of the stockade. Just before we arrived to storm the *pa*, Wiremu Kingi, according to Maori custom, evacuated his 'land title *pa*,' and went off to his fighting fortress. We, under orders, invested the land title *pa*, which we all knew was empty, and at the word of command stormed it gallantly.

"We then put up a land title fortification and returned to New Plymouth. Everything was going on nicely till some members of another tribe, the Ngatiruanui, who were also adversaries of Wiremu Kingi's, murdered some white people to the south of New Plymouth. Had we then gone to Wiremu Kingi, who was a Ngatiawa, and asked him to put off the quarrel about the land, and come and help us punish the Ngatiruanui, all would have been well.

"An expedition was organised, to withdraw our white people from the Southern districts where the murders had taken place,

"The Maoris had built a land title *pa* at Waireka, just on the side of the high-road. It was thought desirable to have the relief party pass round by the sea-coast, whilst the 65th watched the Waireka *pa*.

"When men are sent out to fight Maoris, they should be told what they have to do, and ordered not to return till they have finished it. Colonel Murray, who commanded the 65th, received positive orders to return by nightfall. The Militia and Volunteers who had gone round by the sea-beach fell in with some Maoris and fired on them. An irregular skirmish took place, a great deal of noise was made, and very little harm done. I was in Charley Urquhart's company, and saw the whole proceedings from the top of the hill. When it began to grow dark. Colonel Murray ordered the troops under his command to retire. It was a fine night. The soldiers thought something might turn up in the way of diversion, and as they were scattered about in skirmishing order, it was difficult to collect them together.

"At last they consented to hear the recall, and marched in an irregular manner along the high-road towards New Plymouth.

"On the way they met the sailors who had landed to cut into the sport. We chaffered and hobnobbed with them in the dark, and told them there was an empty *pa* just near the highroad, full of curios and pigs and sport of every kind; and they rushed on. When the sailors got out of the bush, they saw the stockade in the open, and the officers and men all rushed right at it. A few old Maoris, seeing us retire, had returned to the *pa*—which was a land title and not a fighting *pa*—to cook some potatoes. These fired a volley on the sailors, and then ran away. One or two Maoris were killed, and several sailors wounded.

"This was the real cause of the war. These Maoris were Ngatiawa. Few of our people knew one tribe from another. We had attacked Wiremu Kingi's tribe because the Ngatiruanui had murdered our people.

"Wiremu Kingi's people could have murdered all our settlers before morning without difficulty, but did not do so, because, according to Maori custom, the Ngatiawa had no right to erect a stockade on our land. Waireka was our land. We had not only bought it, but cropped it, and held it for many years. The Ngatiawa knew this well, and only put up a stockade as a protest against our occupation of the Waitara. Our farmers who grazed their cattle up to the very line of the Maoris knew it also, and both Maoris and white men used to smoke their pipes in the evening, sitting on the logs around, and some of the white men from a neighbourly feeling helped to hump the heavy timber needed for the corner-posts of that *pa*.

"Well, the newspapers made a great racket about all this, said the 65th had run away, and that had it not been for the bluejackets the whole countryside would have been murdered and New Plymouth sacked.

"We said nothing, but felt *pouri* (Maoris for 'sad'). In a short time, the women and children came in from the out settlements. Not a hair of one of their heads had been touched; not a particle of their furniture, or a single head of their stock had been looted.

"Soon a wing of the 40th Foot arrived from Melbourne, under the command of Major Nelson, and with the Naval Brigade were camped on the Waitara. Communication with this force was kept open by a little steamer, *The Tasmanian Maid*, which crossed the bar of the river, and kept up supplies. All this time the route by land was practically open, and settlers came and went by the Bell Block, as if we were all at peace; but our military commanders either did not know this, or care to admit it. The fact is they were all quarrelling amongst themselves, and nobody knew what the next orders from the governor in Auckland might bring forth.

"Major Nelson was a fiery old field-officer who longed for distinction. He was egged on by Commodore Seymour, who had landed his men, and itched to surpass the achievement of his junior officer who had stormed the Waireka *pa*.

"Major Nelson sent word that he proposed to storm the Puketekauere *pa*, named the day, and warned Colonel Gold, who was the senior officer, to support him by a land march, so as to cut off the retreating Maoris on his left flank. Now, Captain Richards of the 40th Foot had come down as a staff-officer, and when our mess-room was pretty full, swaggered up to the looking-glass, arranged his undress frockcoat, curled his *moustachios*, and said: 'Damn me! There is no *pa* in the country I could not take with my company of Light Bobs.'

"There was no remark made. As soon as he had left, the word was passed round the regiment, 'Captain Richards and the 40th shall have their chance. We will not spoil the sport.'

"When Colonel Gold, who was in command of our regiment, and the senior officer, received Major Nelson's demand for support, he stormed violently, and swore he would forbid the attack. Though he was not aware of Captain Richards' boast—for he was a married officer, and did not frequent our mess—the regiment tipped him the wink; so, he sanctioned the attack, and promised the support.

"Puketekauere was a position of great natural strength. Two small elevations ran into each other, joined by a smooth saddle. The rear and right were protected by a *raupo* swamp. *Raupo* swamps are impassable, though they look inviting. The front was easily approachable even by heavy guns. The left rested on the Waitara River. As is common in river formations, these little eminences had a curve in the middle. They presented the form of an elongated kidney, with its back to the *raupo* swamp. The front hillock was higher and less flat on the top than its fellow, and the bend in the saddle enabled musketry from the lesser hillock to command the approach to the other.

"Major Nelson had no real knowledge of the country or the character of his antagonist. The Maoris built a stockade on the larger hillock, ran up his flag and danced his defiance on the open hillock that led to it. This was more than human nature could stand. Major Nelson fumed and swore until he received the necessary permission from Colonel Gold. He then started off in the dead of the night: Captain Messenger with his Grenadier Company and Lieutenant Brooks with some Light Bobs. The men carried their top-coats, 120 rounds of ammunition, and two days' provision. These were to travel all night, and, at the break of day, to storm the stockade from the rear, as the major with the guns assaulted it from the front.

"Captain Messenger once despatched, the die was cast. There was great preparation, and before dawn off set the main body under Major Nelson and Commodore Seymour with the heavy guns. Nothing but dead silence prevailed. The surprise was complete. The twenty-four pounders, the mortars, and the twelve pounders opened fire. The stockade splintered like matchwood. The assault was ordered, and with a ringing cheer the soldiers and sailors vied with each other to get in first. There was merely a dropping fire from the Maoris, and victory was certain. As soon as our men got up to the stockade, a withering fire was opened from the lesser flanking hillock. The stockade was only a draw. The Maoris had rifle-pitted the whole of the saddle and the lesser hillock.

"As soon as the true position was unmasked, the recall was sounded. The wounded were picked up, the guns were unlimbered. The battle was lost, and for all practical purposes Captain Messenger's force was left to look after itself. The Grenadiers, under Captain Messenger, had at last found the rear of the *pa*. Worn out with fatigue from slaving all night through bush and swamp, they lay down a little to recover themselves. As soon as they heard the firing, up they rose with bounding hearts, and plunged into the swamp as the only road to victory. They threw off their coats, peeled off their tunics, discarded everything but their arms, and pressed on. It was no use.

"It was here Lieutenant Brooks, up to his waist in water, defended himself like a *paladin* with his sword, disabling many an adversary until at length he was tomahawked from behind. Captain Messenger, finding the feat impossible, got together as many of his men as he could, beat to his right, skirted the swamp and rushed the Maori rifle-pits from the rear, where the swamp was more passable, and surprised the Maoris who were looking to their front, engaged with our men. Thus, he carried out his instructions and rejoined the main body, which was in full retreat

"In short, it was a disastrous defeat, and it seems doubtful whether the 40th, which had in the action the flower of its chivalry, will ever get over it. The 65th Foot, under command of Colonel Gold, marched at four o'clock in the morning to cut off the retreat of the Maoris on the left They found the Waingongora River, from recent forest rains in the hills, flooded bank high, and, as they had neither boats nor means for constructing pontoons, they halted, and sought to open communications with Major Nelson by a mounted trooper, whose horse swam the river. This delay did not seem of much importance at the time. Neither was it in reality of any great importance, as it was well known to us that the Maoris, if defeated, would retire up the river to Puke-Rangiora, rather than trust themselves in the open ordinarily accessible to our troops.

"As a matter of fact. Colonel Gold thought Major Nelson had postponed the attack, as he ought to have known by the flooded state of the Waitara that the Waingongora, which served the same watershed, must be impassable to our forces. The general impression in both camps was that Major Nelson had neither expected nor much desired Colonel Gold's co-operation. He meant to score off his own bat, secure a C.B. and a brevet lieutenant-colonelcy, terminate the war to the glory of his own regiment, and return in triumph to his own headquarters in Melbourne."

This is the end of the soldier's story. I gathered it from all branches of Her Majesty's forces, naval, military, volunteers, and militia, and from all ranks of officers and non-commissioned officers engaged in these operations under the grade of field-officer. I have narrated faithfully and without any intentional colouring exactly what I heard, and I knew the intimate thoughts of the soldiers. I belonged to no corps in particular, never having been a regimental officer, and the wounded of all corps came equally under my care. If this narrative should offend anyone, I am sorry. It is the truth as I saw it, and ought to be told.

CHAPTER 5

Entrenched at Waireka

Before proceeding, I ask myself again, what is the object I have in view? Well, I wish to remind the New Zealander of today, whether white or brown, that the Maoris of my time was a gentleman—a man of superior talent and undoubted courage, who knew more about strategy, fortifications, defence and attack than our army had learned either at Woolwich or in India. Also, I would do justice to the British soldier.

Soon after my arrival in New Plymouth, a wing of the 12th regiment, under Major Hutchins, disembarked in the roadstead. A flying column, consisting of some companies of the 12th and 40th, some Royal Engineers and a few artillerymen, was despatched to encamp on the Waireka, the land on which the first engagement between the Maoriss and Volunteers had been fought. I was put in medical charge of the wing. General Pratt was now in command, and all dispositions were carried out with the formality observed in a European campaign. Although we were passing through a peaceable, open, well-cultivated country, skirmishers were thrown out, a rear-guard formed, our baggage waggons were protected by outlying skirmishers, and we proceeded with all possible caution, as though every hedge, hillock, and break concealed a lurking enemy. This had the worst possible effect on the morale of our men, all new to the country.

Arrived at Waireka, we proceeded hastily to entrench ourselves, as if danger was imminent. Before nightfall the lines of our earthworks had been drawn, mounds raised, trenches dug, tents pitched, all within a fortified space. So afraid of a surprise were we that, although we had double pickets out, we had not dared to encamp near either wood or water. In order to secure water from a neighbouring stream, we detached on each occasion an armed party of thirty or forty men to cover the advance and retreat of our water-carriers. Next day we commenced sinking wells. We continued this operation for days. The deeper we sank, the drier the ground, and never once did we turn up either gravel or stone. The soldiers began to think that the devil was in the country.

They had never seen the like before. Finally, the Engineers declared the land waterless, and the fatigue party broke off this work. Our daily expeditions for water were in time extended to search for potatoes. Had it not been for the frequent night-alarms, given by the outlying sentries, followed by the cry, "Man the defences," our lives would have been pleasant enough. All this over-cautious watchfulness had a depressing effect on our men.

By degrees our pickets and scattered handfuls of men went farther afield, until at length many of us began to doubt the existence of any enemy. I made one of these excursions with two or three brother officers. We found on this occasion the body of a farmer which had been shoved into a drain. The settler had been tomahawked in the head, legs, and arms. This was evidently the work of the Ngatiruanui, who were bitterly savage against us. The appearance of this unfortunate man, who had evidently been surprised whilst examining his homestead, gave me "quite a turn."

A few days after this some Maoris appeared in our immediate neighbourhood, and Major Hutchins ordered a reconnaissance. About 150 of our men were thrown into skirmishing order, and instructed to feel their way under cover of some gorse hedges, with the object of getting between the enemy and some neighbouring ridges of elevated land.

It was my duty to accompany the force, and as the troops opened out from the centre and extended to both sides, I found myself on the most distant—the left flank of the line of skirmishers.

As soon as the Maoris saw our object, they opened fire. Our bugles sounded "Take cover." Our men immediately fell flat, crept up anyhow to some gorse hedges, and fired blindly through the fences at anything or nothing. As I lay prone on the ground, clutching absolutely—not figuratively—at the blades of grass, the balls ripped up the sward around me. I first drew in one leg, then another, then tucked in my arm, *anon* tried to bury my head in my shoulders, or my buttock in my back. It was useless. There was no escape. My soul was frozen within me. My orderly. Corporal Prince, was lying beside me. I knew nothing of his state of mind. The bugle sounded. My heart stood still, then the blood bounded back to my brain.

"What is it, Corporal?"

"Call for the medical officer, sir."

"*Malbrouk s'en va-t-en guerre.*" An electric flash went through my brain. Have you the courage to neglect your sacred duty? look in the face of your comrades with the brand of a coward on your heart? No. No. A thousand times no. I arose, alert and smiling. Corporal Prince and I marched with coolness and dignity from one end of the line of skirmishers to the other, almost the only persons exposed to the fire of the enemy. I looked after the wounded without cover and under fire. Now that I had something to do, my fear was gone. The instinct of the doctor was uppermost. The wounded on either side were alike interesting to me. Apparently, if both parties had been firing at me, it would not have made much difference. Training is a wonderful human moulder: I am certain martyrdom is nothing to persons educated to look for it.

As soon as the strength of the Maoris was revealed, the retreat was sounded and our men returned to camp. Very little mischief was inflicted on either side. The range was too long for Maoris smooth-bores. They were chiefly spent balls that frightened the wits out of me. I happened to have been at a point where the fire from two angles converged. The trajectory of our rifles was probably too high to hurt anyone, for the Maoris were up to their chins in rifle-pits.

This little affair left a bad impression on the Maoris. A *reconnaissance en force* seems a fine military exhibition, when defined in words: with the Maoris the mere formal dignity of a withdrawal amounts to nothing. A single Maori as long as he was in view would feel bound in honour to retire with formal dignity, though pursued by a whole army. But ours seemed the retreat of a powerful force. The Maoris concluded we were afraid. Had our men on this occasion been pushed on, and allowed to put their fortunes to the test of battle, it is no exaggeration to say millions of money would have been saved and thousands of lives.

Major Hutchins dared not risk it. Had the attack failed, he would have been cashiered. Had it succeeded, he would have been tried by court-martial and reprimanded. His instructions did not admit of an aggressive movement.

About a week or ten days after this the Maoris, with their women, children, and baggage, were seen pouring over a tortuous mountain quite near us. Their formation was so extended that a company of our men could have destroyed the whole lot. Before Major Hutchins could move a finger, this incident had to be reported in full to head-quarters and then explained and the explanation elucidated.

About four o'clock in the day General Pratt with an overpowering force arrived at our camp. The Maoris had concluded their march about half-past one, and were out of sight over the range of hills. I saw the general and staff on their arrival. They cross-examined every one. My own opinion is they did not believe a word of Major Hutchins's narrative. Maoris cross that range of hills! Where are they? Why, we were in town the whole time, and never saw one of them! The Taranaki volunteers crowded our camp in numbers. Our mess spent about a week's pay feeding them and allaying their thirst. As they went away, I heard them say, "It is a wonder those soldiers cannot fight. They are awfully decent fellows." We all knew their opinion of us, but did not care. Soldiers in any case are hospitable. The rough aspect and cheery familiarity of these volunteers more than compensated us. General Pratt with his formidable force withdrew in an hour or so, and we returned to our usual avocations.

In a few days the Maoris erected earthworks to our left front 800 yards distant, to our left 600 yards distant, and to our left rear about 500 yards. We took no notice of them. One fine morning they opened fire simultaneously from these works. We stood to arms, making no reply except by occasional sharpshooters from our flanking angles. The Maori fire had no effect on us. As our right and right front were open, we continued to draw water from the neighbouring creek and armed parties foraged for potatoes and vegetables coast-wise. We had occasional skirmishes with the enemy, who laid ambuscades for us; but our modes were too uniformly guarded to admit easily of surprises.

Once we surprised an ambuscade consisting of about six or eight Maoris. They all got off, as usual; but one poor fellow, as he was vaulting over a gate 800 yards distant, was caught by an Enfield bullet in an extraordinary way. Our musketry instructor, when running full pelt, dropped on his knee, fixed his sight at 800 yards, pulled the trigger, when down fell the sable warrior. He was up again and bundled off on one leg and two arms whilst you could cry "Jack Robinson," and left nothing behind him except his mat.

The effect of this siege was to restrict our liberty. We had double sentries on our inner defences each night, and were constantly aroused by the firing of our out-pickets. After a little time, everyone got weary of the restraint. Our men began to loaf around outside our fortification, the Maoris firing at them all the time. One day whilst

Major Hutchins was walking about in a fit of affected abstraction, a few of our men began to kick a football. Presently a large portion of the garrison off duty joined in the sport. The Maoris fired volley after volley at our men, but as their distance at this point was 800 yards, not a single shot took effect. They soon left off firing, and looked at us over their rifle-pits. My own opinion is that, had not our men been withdrawn by the sergeants to their evening meal, the Maoris would soon have joined in the game. And certainly, they would have been made welcome. At this time there was no animosity between us. A day or two later the Maoris deserted their position. We were free of the whole country-side, and enjoyed our liberty prodigiously.

Map showing
TRIBAL BOUNDARIES OF THE MAORI
and sites of the
more important engagements of the wars.

English Miles

Loyal Districts (1860-70)....................

Rebel   „   „   ....

Tribal Divisions ....

Tribal Names .... NGAPUHI

CHAPTER 6

Attack on a Stockade

Soon we were ordered to destroy our fortification and retire for the protection of New Plymouth, which was never for a moment in danger. All settlers were ordered within the fortified lines of the town. The women and children were sent to Nelson. Our soldiers were harassed during the long winter nights patrolling a circuit within which a hostile Maoris was never seen. My own experience was that I, in company with three other officers, slept every night about a quarter of a mile outside our farthest pickets in a house belonging to Major Atkinson, and we were never disturbed; but within the fortified area the alarms and precautions were equally great.

As soon as everything was made snug against the surprises of an enemy who was not such a fool as to trust himself miles away from his native forests and ravines, a great expedition was organised against the Maoris camped near the Tataramika block on European land.

The Maori, when he goes on a warlike expedition, casts off all his European clothing. The object is to keep it safe from brambles, when crawling through the forest. Bare-footed and bare-legged, he wears only a flax mat kept by a band which crosses his chest. He carries his double-barrelled gun in one hand, his ammunition in a pouch across his shoulders. His tomahawk he uses as a walking stick. He either carries no food, or, if any, a little fermented maize in a pocket of the mat Thus accoutred, he can do, marching with a loose leg, about five miles an hour, and keep it up on occasion for a long time.

The soldier on the Tataramika expedition carried three days' provisions, a water-bottle in a country where streams were our chief impediment, an overcoat or blanket, or both, 120 rounds of ammunition, a rifle and bayonet As soon as any expedition was over, the N.C. officers checked off all these accoutrements, and if any were missing surcharged the soldier even down to a pair of worn-out socks if lost

The weapon carried was a muzzle-loader, the bullet a tight fit so that much ramming was often necessary. On the march the bayonet when fixed, or when hanging on the hip, was caught in everything. If the rifle was brought to the shoulder, the trajectory of the bullet was too high, failing accurate sighting and steady aim. If fired from the hip, the bullet generally ploughed up the ground about fifteen or twenty yards ahead. The soldier felt he was in a strait waistcoat put up to be fired at by the Maoris. The great expedition appeared miles long. Twenty-four bullocks dragging each a sixty-eight pounder. We had two with us, and were inordinately proud of them. In addition, we had three or four twenty-four pounders and a couple of large mortars. We were quite sure of teaching the Maoris a lesson. Could we only get to the Tataramika, the war would be over in a month or two.

Well, we did get there. We covered each flank of the advancing column with clouds of skirmishers, and they did skirmish, too. I was with them. I wore no impediment but a small Colt's revolver, and I often skirmished on my head and back and hands and knees. As for the progress of the soldier, it was what the Scotch call "just redeeculous."

"Spread yourselves out, men, spread yourselves out," was the cheery order of the officers, as they tumbled about like the rest. It sounded well, and was heard occasionally by the staff-officers; but there was often no room on the cliffs and the breaks to spread in. Thirty Maoris could have surprised in many places any portion of the line, shot the bullocks, crumpled up our arrangements, and laughed at us. The Maoris were, I think, in the neighbouring scrub, smoking their pipes and laughing at us. I do not in the least wonder they did not fire. First, our men were like a lot of children out blackberrying; second, the Maoris had built three lovely *pas*, and wanted us to have a look at them. They knew how easily we were turned back, and in my opinion, had our guns stuck, would have joyously lent a hand under the protection of a flag of truce to extricate our artillery.

They were just as anxious to see the big guns in action as we were. The only difference was: we believed in the arms, the Maoris laughed at them.

Arrived at our goal, we found a lovely plateau, with a fringe of forest lining its inland margin. We pitched our tents with their backs to the sea, hauled our guns to our front, and despatched a large fatigue party to run up light earthworks on our right and left. The staff-officers galloped about, took hurried sketches, measured distances, and consulted together. It was much more interesting than any review I had ever seen. There were three stockades on the edge, as it were, of a large oval dish. The only curious feature was that from our position we could only see the tops of forest trees. There were no bowls or stems of trees visible. The foliage just rocked and played in the light sea breeze.

The staff seemed puzzled which of the three stockades to attack. There was not a Maori to be seen. Finally, it was decided to attack the central stockade, and keep the others under observation. The sixty-eights, twenty-fours, and mortars opened fire. The skirmishers on the right and left lay flat on the ground. It was magnificent; it was war at last. An occasional Maori sharpshooter picked off one of our men, otherwise there was no reply from the *pa*. We hammered this stockade for twenty-four hours. At length the engineers, after an examination with their binoculars, announced a practical breach. There was a hush and a stir. The storming party was told off. The distance was certainly not more than 400 yards. The word was given.

Suddenly there rose up from the ground about 120 men. If you have ever seen hounds, whilst still fresh, rush at a fox near in sight, all in a cluster, straining against each other for first place, such was the storming party. It was a mercy from heaven there were no Maoris in the *pa*. Children with arms in their hands could have mown our men down by dozens. Arrived at the stockade, though unopposed, there was no one soldier could get in for some time. The Maoris had rifle-pitted the earth in front of the palisade. The rifle-pits had arched roofs of green timber covered with soft earth and fern. On the level of the plateau a sort of open wickerwork window, from four to six inches deep, lit up and ventilated the rifle-pits. The Maoris had stood inside the rifle-pits, poked their fowling-pieces through the wicker window, and pulled the trigger without exposing themselves. That was the reason why all our wounded men were hit in the legs. From these rifle-pits covered galleries led to the rear, and were lost in the forests.

Not a single shell or round-shot had entered these rifle-pits. The whole of our fire, so far as the Maoris were concerned, was merely a pyrotechnic display. The stockade was crescent-shaped, lost itself at each end in a sharp declivity. It had been built of young forest trees with the sap in them. They were fixed upright in the ground, and branches were lashed across with green flax. The space between the double row of cross saplings was filled with loose earth. Our shot and shell had passed clean through. The jagged, shattered timber merely waggled about once it was broken, held in position above and below by green flax ties. Undefended, and all as it was, none of our men succeeded in getting either over or through the stockade until the sappers came along with axes and cut through the flax lashings.

The British soldier is not much of a fool. He was strictly forbidden to stray from the main body, and the storming party was recalled without being allowed to explore the *pa*. But the storming party had seen quite enough, and graphically detailed their observations. Forthwith the commanders, staff-officers, and engineers were looked on with profound contempt. A panic seemed to have seized the general. If the Maoris have deserted their works, when and why? How shall we ever get back to New Plymouth? There are defiles on the road where a few hundred men could destroy a whole army.

On our retreat nearly the whole of the force was thrown into skirmishing order to protect our guns and baggage. We got back to New Plymouth in safety, and hid ourselves behind our stockades, which, by the way, were so extended as to be nearly useless. A body of irregular horsemen could certainly have broken through them.

It was at Tataramika that I saw the following illustration of the value of our small arms. We had a handful of sailors from the Naval Brigade along with us. They were armed with Colt's naval revolvers and sabres. Sailors ashore are the jolliest fighting men imaginable. They, of course, expected to be joined in the assault when the happy moment came, and they set to work to prepare their implements of war. At that time Colt's revolvers required caps. The nipples for the caps were small and fine. The sailor's thumbs and fingers are coarse, the skin thick, and the sense of touch blunted.

This was the procedure. The sailor sat on his hunkers, steadied the revolver between his two big-toes, and then, with the aid of two pins, one in each hand, put the cap on each nipple. When I saw this, and viewed the sailor's humorous contempt for the size of the revolver bullet, I quite believed what I had heard of the sailors who had helped to storm Puketekaure under Commodore Seymour.

My informant assured me the sailors first emptied all the chambers of their revolvers, then threw them away, and, yelling out "Board!" drew their sabres and rushed at the stockade.

CHAPTER 7

Sir Donald McLean's Story

The following narrative was related to me by Sir Donald McLean, the greatest Maori scholar of our time, with the single exception of Judge Maning, the author of *Old New Zealand*, who in curious lore was probably Sir Donald's superior. In variety of useful political knowledge and general acquaintanceship with the outer life of the various tribes, Sir Donald McLean was without an equal. Donald was a Highlander, about six feet two inches, with a broad, expansive chest, a flat, strong forehead, a blue-grey, open eye, a genial manner, and an affectionate nature. All this was dominated by an ambitious temper, and the wonderful Scottish talent for economy and reticence.

A chat with Sir Donald would convince anyone that he was a guileless character. He was, too, in a sense. His influence with the Maoris was due to his imperturbability. He could beat them at their own game of "*Taihoa*" (*i.e.* "Wait a bit"). Yet he was a most touchy, irritable, excitable man. When he had a little whisky in, and was at ease with his company—which on such occasions never included a Maoris—Donald would jump on the table and dance a Highland sword-dance with blazing enthusiasm.

What a race these Scots are! What a fine fellow in his heart and brain was our Sir Donald!

In order to guarantee Sir Donald's story of Waitini, I want you to see the Scotchman at work. Donald McLean was Native Land Purchase Commissioner.

Land for settlement was indispensable. Often the Maoris would not sell, yet if you gave Sir Donald his own time and did not interfere the land was always bought.

Donald seduced the Maoris into talking the proposal over—just a *korero* (debate). He sent the chiefs some flour and sugar, passed round the word among all the neighbouring *hapus* (tribes) that at such a time "there would be a talk about the land."

Maori custom made it indispensable for a great chief to entertain all guests. All the Maoris, no matter how distantly related, congregated to hear the talk (*korero*). Some of them travelled hundreds of miles, and came accompanied by their wives and children. The great chiefs were thus eaten out of house and home, and had no alternative but to sell the land. There was one inveterately obstinate chief who would do nothing. A great *korero* was engineered against him. He was the only rich man left. He could not get out of the *korero*. His *mana* (*i.e.* prestige) was at stake. Donald McLean had nothing to do with engineering the *korero*. Oh dear, no. Donald's *mana* was also at stake. This Maori was not a queen's native. He was a turbulent outsider. Donald would have nothing to say to him in the way of business. The *hapus* crowded in from all sides. The rich man had plenty; he did not care. He was a great chief; in any case he meant to show his power.

After a little time, the tempter said, "A great chief like you ought not to be afraid of a mere queen's servant (*cookie*) like Donald McLean. Let him be invited, that he may do homage to our *Tino Rangatira.*"

Donald was asked to the feast. Donald sat and smoked and listened for three months. The *Tino Rangatira* could not turn him away. Such a course was against all rules. The others could not leave till Sir Donald left. It would be underbred to do so; besides, they were comfortable where they were. Not a word ever came out of Donald's mouth about the land. He narrated legends of the fallen greatness of the various *hapus* and tribes, and acquired an intimate knowledge of the personal history of every man of importance present.

In an ordinary conversation he would say, "By the bye, Piri Piri, do you remember when you were crossing a branch of the Opotiki River in the Whakatane district in the month of April, '54—I think it was on a Wednesday. When cooling your foot (which you had struck against a jagged stump of rata) in the mudhole, you were bitten by a large crayfish, and thought it was the '*Taniwha*'?"

Now, Piri Piri, who was an utter stranger to McLean, and had travelled hundreds of miles to be present at the *Runanga*, was duly impressed. In time, many of the Maoris from distant parts began to think that McLean had the second sight (McLean had, of course, learned Piri Piri's story from the Whakatane natives.) Before such a power the influence of the *Tino Rangatira* began to wane. In addition, his provisions were beginning to run low. His money was all gone, his credit was suffering, and yet there was no sign of movement from McLean. The Maoris have a great gift of humour, which is not infrequently associated with good sense. The *Tino Rangatira* came to McLean and said, "For God's sake, take the land and go home."

Donald did take the land, and there was a flourishing settlement on it within five years. The *Tino Rangatira* had all his debts paid, and the remainder of the land was doubled in value by the nearer approach of civilization. This chief proved a great friend of ours in the troublous times, and, as he was a gentleman, a strategist, a Maori, and a man of honour, held McLean in the greatest esteem for ever after. He knew that McLean had outwitted him by his astuteness and business acumen, and as there was no trick in the game, he bore Donald no ill-will.

NGA WIREMU TAMIHANA

THE KING MAKER

CHAPTER 8

Waitini and Wiremu Kingi

Here is Donald McLean's story about Waitini:—

There was much tribal jealousy between the Ngatiawa and the Ngatimaniopoto, two neighbouring tribes. This was before the natives acquired fire-arms. It was the custom then to fight in *phalanx*, just as the Greeks did. The two tribes were drawn up in battle array, distant from each other about eight hundred yards. Neither was anxious to begin the fight. They were too equally matched, and embarrassing intermarriages had taken place during a long peace.

Waitini was a Ngatiawa of the purest blood. With great dignity he stepped out of his *phalanx*, and marched half the distance towards the Ngatimaniopoto. There he halted, sang his song, flourished his tomahawk, slapped his buttock, and strutted defiantly about.

Three young Ngatimaniopoto chiefs rushed out from their *phalanx* to capture Waitini. As they started abreast, straining every nerve, Waitini sat down to pick a thorn out of his foot. Waitini apparently saw nothing, and, as his adversaries approached, a dreadful yell was sent up to heaven by his tribe, who saw his danger. He moved not a muscle. He was lost. An ominous silence fell upon his people; their hearts were bursting with alarm. The reckless Waitini continued to pick at the thorn; his tomahawk even was laid listlessly by his side.

Waitini had calculated all the chances. It was a brave man's lure. The Ngatimaniopoto were of unequal speed. There was, however, but little distance between them. The first was on Waitini apparently before he woke up. He did wake up, however, sprang like a panther half to one side, and then swung round. His youthful adversary could not check his speed, and, as he passed, Waitini buried his hatchet in the Ngatimaniopoto's skull.

The second man was on him almost before he could clear his axe. Waitini ran for his life at a right angle to his adversaries' course. The two Ngatimaniopoto followed him, the foremost making a bee-line, the next at an oblique angle. Waitini fell on his knee when he was all but caught. The first pursuer stumbled over him, and met his death as he fell. Waitini then rushed at the third adversary, whose eye quailed for a moment in doubt. In the moment of indecision, he was slain. The two *phalanxes* then rushed at each other in great fury. Waitini, with coolness, waited for his men. The Ngatimaniopoto were beaten. There was great slaughter, and the Ngatiawa became the dominant tribe, and remained so until the downfall of the King movement.

It is easy to understand the character and position of a man like Waitini amongst such a race. He was worthy of it all—genial, kindly, unassuming, brave; and what a hero he looked! He was six foot four, twenty-one stone weight, without a particle of spare flesh on him. I saw him naked. He had muscles like iron bands, a head like a Roman emperor, and a heart in loyalty and simplicity like a child's.

When the great wave of enthusiasm for national independence swept over Maorisdom, Waitini, with a chosen band of 140 men, went down to Taranaki to fight for the cause.

Waitini Taiporutu was a sucking babe in Wiremu Kingi's hands. Wiremu Kingi was a diplomatist. He was amongst the Maoris a counsel chief; that is, a politician. Waitini Taiporutu was a war chief, a soldier.

Wi Tamihana te Waharoa was a counsel chief of the Ngatiawa, Waitini's tribe. Tamihana besought Waitini not to go to the Taranaki war.

You are a great warrior. We cannot spare you. The trouble is coming home to us. I see it. You are a great baby, too—guileless as an innocent girl. You are my sister's son and the pride of your race. Wiremu Kingi is a subtle, white man's Maoris, without any special sense of honour. He will entrap you, and you will be lost. You weaken our tribe by taking away the pick of our young men; and when it is all over, the Ngatimaniopoto will turn and rend us. The future of our race is in your hands; stand fast, and wait. In due time, I will find you fighting enough.

193

In spite of it all, Waitini would go to the war. The fever was in his blood.

THE BATTLE OF MAHOETAHI

Mahoetahi lay about five or six miles to the north of New Plymouth. It was a knoll with sides sloping irregularly. Somewhat egg-shaped, it was almost surrounded by a flax and *raupo* swamp. It was easily approachable on the north-east, where a dry ridge led from the open plain right up to the brow of the knoll.

When Waitini arrived at Waitara and joined forces with Wiremu Kingi, he carried things with a high hand. Haperona, a slave by birth, was Wiremu Kingi's fighting chief, a little, fiery man, with a jealous temper and great military talent On Waitini's arrival, Haperona was relegated to an insignificant position. Wiremu Kingi was a man of imagination, with a practical turn for affairs.

He was not carried away by any Utopian idea of Maori nationality. He had lived too long among white men of high intellectual order to deceive himself. He was at Waikanae the personal friend of Archdeacon Hadfield, a distinguished missioner, who had been educated at one of our great English Universities. Archdeacon Hadfield united to great enthusiasm for the Church scholarly attainments of a high character. He was by nature meant for a constitutional lawyer. Divine faith turned him into an apostle. Wiremu Kingi sat at his feet, and became an enthusiast for the British Constitution. Wiremu was forced into war by Governor Gore Brown's pragmatic incapacity.

Kingi had sufficient intellectual power to command a large following in the Parliament of the colony. Isaac Earle Featherston, William Fox, William Fitzherbert, Archdeacon Hadfield, and Bishop Selwyn were the advocates of his views. Wiremu had used the wave of Maori enthusiasm to further his purpose and secure allies in men and money, but he had no intention of being swallowed up in the King movement. Therefore, Waitini Taiporutu's arrival was to him by no means an unmixed blessing. To make war for the defence of his tribal land and constitutional privileges as a British subject, with the whole of Exeter Hall and half the New Zealand Parliament at his back, was one thing; to declare openly for the Maori king another. Wiremu Kingi dissembled. He said to Waitini:

> Hitherto we have done nothing. Now indeed, with the chivalry of Waikato, under the command of our greatest soldier, we can make a forward movement, and drive the *Pakeha* into the sea.

Waitini, accompanied by Haperona, and a few of his own tribe, scouted for a day or so. Finally, they agreed to establish a post at Mahoetahi, on a part of the land in dispute, and challenge General Pratt to a pitched battle, beat him, and then by a forced march along the sea-shore cut him from his communications with the sea.

For this purpose it was agreed that Waitini, with his Waikato warriors, was to hold Mahoetahi as a blind; the soldiers, who had always acted like fools, were to be drawn on to make an attack on the front and sides of the knoll through the swamp; and that Haperona, with 800 armed men, was to cover, if necessary, Waitini's retreat. On the morning of the battle, Waitini in person made all the dispositions. He planted Haperona, with his 800 men, in some scrub to the north-east of the ridge which led up to Mahoetahi, where these men lay absolutely hidden. He supported them with 400 men under the personal command of Wiremu Kingi.

These were hidden in a wooded gulch, half a mile to the rear of Haperona's position. Waitini was to stand singly the assault. When he was surrounded in the agony of the struggle, Haperona was to extend his men fan-shaped to the right and left, take our forces by surprise in the rear; then, at a given signal, Wiremu Kingi was to move rapidly to his right front by the seacoast, and cut off General Pratt's retreat to New Plymouth.

I have never been able to satisfy myself as to the cause of the absolute failure of this combined movement. Either Wiremu Kingi's courage failed him at the supreme moment, which is quite possible, as he was only a counsel chief, or Haperona, out of pique, determined to destroy Waitini, or there was an agreement from the beginning between Wiremu Kingi and Haperona to humble the Waikato. From personal acquaintanceship with Haperona, I am inclined to think that he merely obeyed Wiremu Kingi's orders, whatever they were. Haperona had military genius and a profound contempt for the soldier. His position was a perfectly safe one, practically chosen by himself. His chief also was out of danger, his rear being covered with capable scouts in touch with his fighting *pas*. Whatever the cause, Waitini Taiporutu was not assisted in the hour of danger, and the flower and chivalry of Waikato was left to perish at Mahoetahi.

HAPERONA

CHAPTER 9

General Pratt at Mahoetahi

Before describing the battle, I wish to sketch for you the state of things in New Plymouth. General Pratt had received a distinct challenge to fight the quarrel out signed by Waitini, Wiremu Kingi, and Haperona. One Maori name was as good to him as another. The whole war was in his judgment one vast nightmare. The general was a tall, weakly old man, who suffered habitually from diarrhoea. He sat his horse like a soldier, and was above personal timidity. An austere phlegm was the varnish with which nature concealed a feeble and irresolute will. He was a gentleman anxious to do his duty, but the marrow had long since gone out of his bones. He was surrounded by an active, capable staff who only worried him; but in the end he did whatever he was told. He consented to accept the challenge, and ordered the necessary preparations.

The morning of the 6th November (1860) was cool and a bit dark. The soldiers paraded in the main street of the town. It looked an imposing force. The Taranaki volunteers were intended to act as supports, and space was left in the column for their companies. When the force was ready to march, as the space retained for Taranaki volunteers was not nearly filled, there was much tittering and ridicule amongst the soldiers. Colonel Carey rode up to Major Atkinson, and said,—

"Major, this is very bad. Where are your men?"

Major Atkinson was a stumpy little Devonshire man, with a long body, short legs, shaggy eyebrows, and an eye betokening a highly intellectual character. His brain was so hot within his head that his coarse, short hair always stood up. He was the gentlest of men and the bravest of soldiers. In battle, or when he was angry, Harry Atkinson's eye wore the cold, fierce glitter of the wild boar. His eye now shone with a fierce light, as he replied in a hoarse trumpet voice that penetrated one's bones,—

"Colonel, let the column advance. My men will fall in as we go, and, in any case, there are enough volunteers present to storm the position."

This savage answer electrified the listeners.

I watched Colonel Carey's face. He was a *débonnaire* little man, as brave as a bantam cock, shrewd as a court bailiff. He smiled good-naturedly. Everyone knew the serious side of Major Atkinson's character. Colonel Carey alone saw the grotesque. The news of the major's defiant air spread like wildfire through the settlement. His men joined the column in threes and fours as we marched along, and soon the major's complete companies were in the ranks.

The interview with Major Atkinson was reported to General Pratt, who smiled in grim content. Great was his animosity against the volunteers (though his was a kindly nature) because the *Taranaki Herald* had held him and his soldiers up to unmeasured contempt. He felt that at last each was to occupy its proper relative position in the public view, and that this parade had drawn the sting of volunteer ridicule.

Arrived at Mahoetahi, the general saw nothing but an insignificant hill surrounded with an apparently dry swamp. There was not a Maori to be seen, nor an earthwork or stockade. The only sign of life was a thin wreath of smoke ascending peaceably in the morning air.

The general chewed his grey moustache, eased himself by sitting sideways in the saddle, and said,—

"Well, Carey, sold again?"

Just as they were in doubt, Major Atkinson fell out of the ranks, and, hot with seething emotions, walked up to the general, and said,—

"General, my men were slow in parading. This is our land. I claim for the Taranaki volunteers the honour of the assault"

The general looked at Colonel Carey, who said,—

"Major, the dispositions for the attack are not yet completed. In any case you and your men are entitled to an honourable position in the field. You shall hear from the general later."

It was then decided that the assault should be entrusted to a company of the 65th Foot, and a company of the Taranaki volunteers under the command of Major Atkinson. A wiser decision could not have been arrived at. Both of these forces knew the country well.

Instructions were given for the various companies to deploy to the right and the left, so as to surround Mahoetahi. Major Nelson at Waitara had been warned by marching early to take it in the rear. The guns unlimbered were brought into position, and commenced firing. The 65th and Taranaki volunteers, skirmishing around, soon found practical access at the rear. With great fury they hurled themselves at the elevated ridge, where they were met by Waitini in person leading his men.

Here a hand-to-hand conflict between the tomahawk and the bayonet took place in the open. Both the natives and the white men were too eager to reload once the first volley was fired. Waitini was both outnumbered and overmatched in weapons. His men went down in numbers, Waitini amongst the very first.

When the ridge was carried, the remainder of Waitini's men took to the swamp, and in many instances were hunted like rats in a waterhole. Many of them got away into the high fern, before our soldiers woke up to the realisation of the victory.

Haperona at Waitini's rear merely fired a volley in the air and decamped. The bitter story of Waitini's death was told with weeping all over the Waikato, and the Waikatos swore eternal vengeance for a near day.

The confusion amongst our men was great. There were so few Maoris to kill, and so many anxious to kill them. This incident caught my eye. A noble-looking Maori, naked and tattooed, stood up to his waist in swamp-water. He was quite near, and flourished his tomahawk bravely. The Enfield rifle was a beast of a weapon at a short range. The trajectory was too high. In the haste and turmoil many of our men fired at him, but missed. A hot-headed Irishman, impatient of the delay, took a running jump, and with fixed bayonet made a rush at him. The Maori, as he saw his adversary in the air, lightly stooped, and let his tomahawk swing to his wrist by its thong. The bayonet passed over his head, and he caught the soldier by the hips and waist, and gently placed him under his foot in the water. There was a furious shout from the bank, "He is drowning Mick Ryan."

Two or three men lay on their stomachs, and fired point-blank. As the gallant Maori toppled over, Mick came to the surface spluttering, and bawled out, "Bedad, I thought he had smothered me entirely, entirely."

As soon as the battle was over, we gathered together the Maori dead. Wounded Maoris there were none. None of the dead were mutilated. To the number of fifty the Waikatos got off through the swamp and fern. The gallant dead were carted into New Plymouth on our gun-carriages. There they were all laid out like pheasants after a *bat-*

tue. Descriptions of their tattoos, with full details of their height and figure, were taken down, and published in the Maori language. There was to be no mistake about the announcement of the victory.

And a victory it was, though it brought us much trouble, and finally led to the Waikato war. The escaped Ngatiaua (Waikatos), after the manner of their race, graphically told the whole story on their return home. These are the only particulars I have to add.

When Waitini's scouts ran in and said, "The soldiers are approaching," Waitini, with Maori stolidity, replied, "Waitini is at his breakfast." When informed that the soldiers had arrived, he said, "Waitini is at his breakfast." When assured the whole position was surrounded, he rose, and quietly said, "Waitini has finished his breakfast." Then at the head of his men he rushed to meet the storming party, which had already touched the crown of the hill.

One word in extenuation of Wiremu Kingi's desertion of his noble ally.

It is undoubtedly true that Major Nelson's march from Waitara took Wiremu Kingi by surprise, because it threatened his rear. It had never been calculated by Waitini, when he made his dispositions, that so important a concentration could be effected.

It is difficult to acquit Wiremu Kingi, however, of a full knowledge of our resources, and certain it is in my opinion that Wiremu Kingi would never have deserted his own people as he did the Waikatos. When the details of the catastrophe were sifted at Ngaruawahia by the King's Council, it was resolved, in the interests of the Maori national movement, to hush up the facts; but the sting remained, and had it not been for the necessity of combining against the common (English) foe the treachery would have been wiped out in blood

CHAPTER 10

A Military Hospital

Shortly after the affair of Mahoetahi I was moved up to Waitara, and placed in charge of the field hospital there. My intimacy with the officers of the flying column, under Major Hutchins, was thus broken off. I found myself a stranger; and, as I had no regimental ties, I lived a good deal alone, and mouched about amongst our outposts, making a study of the British soldier. I found him to be very much as circumstances made him. The 65th man was a breezy, brawny giant, who moved about in loose clothes, open, chatty, and good-natured. He got blazing drunk whenever the opportunity offered, took his punishment next day as if it were a cup of coffee, was a perfectly wholesome child of nature, who laughed and shook hands with every one he met. He was perfectly respectful to his officer, saluted him reverently with a twinkle in his eye, as though he would say, "How goes it, Charley?"

The 40th man was a perfect beauty. The best set up soldier I had ever seen, clean and smart, he was secretly bitterly discontented. He had come from Melbourne, where he had been the pride of the parks and the joy of Collins Street. He was a citizen in his tastes, hated the mud and rain of this d——d country, and daily longed for his discharge, so that he might return to Melbourne.

The 12th man was less showy than the 40th soldier and more contented. He was a bit languid, and enjoyed the fresh air after the enervating heat of Sydney. The sailors were all alike, except that the detachment from the Royal *Colonial* steam sloop-of-war *Victoria*, which received a high colonial wage and was never flogged, seemed to think little of itself, and was good-naturedly tolerated by the Royal Jack-tar, whose pay was very small, and discipline of a bitterly rigid character. When a Jack was triced up to the triangle and received four dozen, the colonial sailors seemed to hang their heads, and the Jack-tars swelled

201

with natural pride. "That's how we do it in the Royal Navy." "Poor miserable beggars! There is not an officer amongst you dare flog a man, nor a sailor that is worth it."

The chief military duty at that time consisted of outpost work. I noticed that the men of the 40th and 12th regiments came in jaded and weary, whilst the soldiers of the 65th Foot always turned up in the morning fresh and rosy. I was much struck with this difference, which was more marked in rough, wet weather. The temperaments of the men accounted for part of it; but the difference was so glaring I determined to inquire into the cause.

I asked a 65th man for an explanation. He said, "We are on duty tonight. The weather is wet and cold. Come round to our outposts after 'grand rounds' and see for yourself."

I did so. The outposts had been inspected, all orders were given for the night. The officer on duty had retired within the lines. I crept up and was recognised by the men. A soldier near me on sentry called out in a loud drawling voice, "Tena koe?" (Maori for "How are you?"). Immediately long spun out, "Tena koutou?" ("How are you all?") was heard.

The soldier replied, "Tena koutou oeto" ("God save you all").

The Maori replied, "Kapai te Hickety Pifth" (65th). "Good, it is the sixty-fifth regiment."

The soldier answered, "Kapai te Maoris" ("Good, it is the Maoris").

The Maori said, "Too wet and cold tonight. Let us all go to sleep."

The soldier replied, "All right." Certain it is there was no firing. Each relied on the other's honour. Had there been any change of policy, the Maoris would assuredly have given full notice.

CHAPTER 11

Peach-Groves and Thistles

On receipt of information that the Maoris had deserted their *pa*, and were digging potatoes and collecting peaches in a small but beautiful valley, we determined to surprise them. In order to do so, we started off two hours before the break of day, about 1,000 of us, with as much clatter and noise as if we were going to market. Having marched for miles through tangled fern, we arrived at a slope of ground fringed with forest. A halt was called, and our guide and interpreter was sent for. Colonel Carey questioned the interpreter in my hearing.

"Yes, there are the peach-groves," he said. "But you told me there was an open plain."

"So, there was. Owing to neglect of the land since this war broke out, this forest of thistles has grown up."

Colonel Carey looked incredulous—the general weary and disgusted. Skirmishers were thrown out, and ordered to enter this cover. I rode a pony about fourteen hands three high. It was my duty to accompany the skirmishers, and I did not dismount. It was with difficulty I forced my horse through the thistles, such was the closeness and strength of the growth. The horse's skin was not pricked, because he had to do merely with the stem. I got all the benefit of the thorns. As I rode, the thistles were up to my shoulders. They were ordinary Scotch thistles, accidentally imported in grass-seed, flourishing in a virgin soil. Who after this can wonder at the success of Scotchmen in a new country? I am aware there are persons who, on perusal, will consider this account of the growth of thistles exaggerated. I have nothing to do with such. It is my mission to tell the truth as I saw it

When the little battle was over—the Maoris were there—we had to tell off a large fatigue party with bill-hooks to cut a road through the thistles. The crop was as thick as wheat, yielding forty bushels to the acre, and the uncut sides offered a solid barrier to any entrance except by force.

The Rev. Mr. Wilson, a charming Church of England missionary, accompanied us on the expedition. He was a simple-minded, sincere, delightful companion. He had been a chaplain in H.M. Navy, and left the service to Christianise the Maoris. We became great friends. As it was reported we had killed and wounded many of the Maoris who were too proud to desert their peach-groves without a fight, Mr. Wilson decided to pay them a visit of condolence. I volunteered to accompany him, to look after the wounded. He said he would first go alone, and then, if the Maoris consented, return for me.

He did return. His reception had been friendly; but they denied having any wounded, and added, if there were, their own doctor was sufficient for their purposes. Mr. Wilson was rather sad, foreseeing that the war would end badly. We cut down all the peach trees, dug up the potatoes, devastated the country (as far as its nature would permit), and returned to our camp at Waitara.

CHAPTER 12

Maoris Surprise Attacks

On the 28th December another expedition was organised. We marched in great silence at two o'clock in the morning, and arrived at Mate-Riko-Riko at dawn.

It was a lovely morning. The languid summer air, moistened by evaporating dew, soothed our weary limbs as we lay stretched on the ground. I was on duty with the advanced guard. I was a complete stranger both to officers and men, and had not even selected an orderly. With a few surgical appliances in my haversack and some ship biscuits in the pocket of my blue jumper, I rested apart under the shelter of a clump of fern. The men had stacked their arms, and were lying about smoking. Their officers (I think) had returned to their regimental headquarters for a hurried breakfast. I listened to the conversation of the soldiers.

They were discussing the folly and absurdity of the whole war, declaiming against the injustice which bound them to a service for a shilling a day, subject to stoppages, whilst a useless volunteer received half a crown a day and full liberty to disobey orders if he liked. Public opinion in the advance guard verged on sedition, when suddenly, like a transformation scene in a pantomime, the Maoris were amongst us. I was stricken with terror and dazed with admiration. The Maoris, with their tongues out, eyes starting out of their heads, jumping from side to side like panthers, flourishing their tomahawks, shaking the feathers of their *taias* in our very noses, presented a dreadful spectacle.

Our men rose in a panic, rushed to their stacked arms, which were unloaded, and clean bolted. A few men were wounded at my feet. One in particular, shot in the thigh and bleeding profusely, looked in my face with the eye the sheep casts on the butcher as the knife is descending. Great God! what was I to do?" If I remained, I would be tomahawked. Desert the wounded man I could not. Suddenly I had an inspiration.

I jumped up from the side of the stricken soldier, fired one barrel of my revolver at the nearest Maori, and yelled out, "Tipperary to the rescue!"

The running soldiers turned like a flock of starlings.

"Give them the point of the bayonet, boys!" I shouted.

The revulsion was immediate. One great yell, "Tipperary!" went up to heaven. The Maoris disappeared like a bad dream, and I made off with my wounded.

It is true, so great for the moment was the panic, I had to stop some of the retreating men with my pistol, and force them to carry off the wounded. For this little service I was introduced by a singularly gallant man, our chief medical officer, to the general for notice in despatches. I was all dishevelled, my hands and clothes stained in blood. The general said: "He is too young to mention in despatches. At the least, he might have washed his hands."

I was not such a fool as to expect to be mentioned in despatches. The fact was, I had rallied the men to save myself and the wounded; and as soon as I could, I got out of danger. There was no particular bravery in my conduct. You cannot praise a non-combatant officer for rallying soldiers without degrading combatant officers. In this case there was no combatant officer present. Was the general likely to confess such a breach of discipline? I held my tongue scrupulously, and the whole incident was passed over as though it had never happened. All the same, the chief medical officer came to me a few days later, and said:—

"You shall accompany the next assaulting party. It is going to be a serious affair, and, if you come out of it all right, 'you shall be mentioned in despatches.' The general has promised it."

I experienced a cold dull down my spinal column. I thought, "Damn your despatches!"

I said, "Understand, I will do anything I am ordered; but, in my opinion, no glory is worth a bullet wound."

He, who was covered with medals, and wore the Victoria Cross, looked at me with scarcely smothered contempt He was never as friendly afterwards.

The general changed his mind about the assault. Perhaps, if it had come off, I would not have been detailed for that duty. The surprise at Mate-Riko-Riko, with other considerations, changed the whole conduct of the Taranaki war. The general made up his mind to approach Wiremu Kingi's fighting *pa*, Puke-Rangiore, by sap. The occupation of Mate-Riko-Riko left its front open to us. We made clear our base of operations by making a roadway one chain wide all the way to Waitara. The lesson afforded by the evacuated Tataramika *pa*, previously described, lived in the general's mind. He decided no fighting *pa* was practicable for a storming party. An earthwork with flanking angles was thrown up. Our ammunition and provisions were placed in this under a strong guard. All the fern and scrub near us was cleared away. Double pickets were placed in various directions. Double sentries patrolled all night.

We then advanced about 400 yards by sap, rolling before us a huge gabion (wicker roller). Then we erected another redoubt—an earthwork with flanking angles. In this we encamped about 150 men. Double sentry duty was enforced inside each of these works all night.

We then pushed on our sap about 400 yards. All this advancing was, of course, daily and hourly resisted by the Maoris.

Here we erected a large earthwork, without flanking angles, to accommodate 300 men. It was called No. 3 redoubt. The precautions at this point were redoubled, because the ridge on which we were advancing fell away here to the left, and was lost in a gentle slope about fifteen yards distant from our fortification. There had been some discussion about the wisdom of construction without flanking angles, but, as the force was so large and time an element of importance, it was determined to hurry on. It was considered quite safe, as our men occupied at this time the head of the sap each night.

From this point the sap proceeded more slowly, as every inch of the ground was disputed by the Maoris. We erected in time No. 4 redoubt, to contain 150 men; and Nos. 5 and 6 redoubts, with flanking angles, containing together about 600 men.

We were now about 250 yards from the Puke-Rangiore *pa*, well within range of the Maori rifle-pits, yet our precautions were such that we scarcely ever had a man wounded.

Our safe and near approach aggravated the Maoris beyond endurance. Having received reinforcements from Waikato, in the shape of a body of men who came to seek *utu* (revenge) for Waitini Taiporutu's death, the Maoris determined to assume the offensive.

Our six redoubts were in exact line. All of them were of the same width. Thus, every flanking angle within rifle range commanded the approach to its neighbour's side. Therefore No. 3 redoubt, though unprovided with flanking angles, had its approach on the sides protected by Nos. 2 and 4 redoubts. Each redoubt projected its earthen wall about five feet above the level of the ground, and was surrounded by a ditch about four feet deep and proportionately wide.

The Maoris picked a storming party of 130 men. They crept along one very dark night till they came to No. 3 redoubt, where the land sloped off to the left of our earthwork. Here each Maori singly crept on his belly till he got into the ditch, where in time the whole storming party lay breathlessly still.

Lieutenant Jackson of the 40th was the officer on duty for the night. The sentry reported that there was some scratching noise going on in the ditch. Lieutenant Jackson got on the top of the earthen wall and peered over. He said to the sentry—

"There is nothing. It is all quiet. It is as dark as pitch."

The sentry replied, "I did hear something, sir."

Jackson said, "Hold me hard by the legs; I will reach down and see. I do not want to alarm the camp."

As Jackson leant further over, an impatient Maori shot him through the head

The sentry roared out, "Man the defences!"

Immediately the Maoris in the ditch swarmed over. They had cut steps in the earthen wall with their axes. Our men all slept in their clothes, with their arms stacked hard by. The Maoris were met by the bayonet. One Maori, as he was mounting the ditch, was run through the body. He seized the soldier's rifle in both hands. The soldier never thought of letting go, and, as the Maori and soldier were thus fixed, the Maoris crept over their wounded comrade's back.

In the meantime, the assaulting party's allies commenced a furious attack on the front, sides, and rear of No. 6 redoubt. It was all futile. The men from Nos. 1, 4, and 5 redoubts hurried up at the double, and took the Maoris on each flank. The affair was over in a few moments, and, as usual, the Maoris left very few wounded or killed on the field. Of course, the darkness of the night favoured the escape.

Indeed, in any case, live shells constantly thrown into the ditch made the Maori position at No. 3 untenable, and, as surprise was the essence of the scheme, the storming party at once gave up the enterprise. By this time all the friendship between the races was over. We were in the death-grips with each other. The Maoris knew our military customs perfectly. We had never once been caught asleep, yet they backed their gallantry against all our precautions, and expected to cut our whole force in two in the middle of the night. Not often was a braver military achievement attempted.

Were I to try and describe to you the agonising shame the Maoris experienced at this defeat, I should suffer too much. Suffice it to say, the wounded and dying could not lift up their heads. They kept on declaring they were cowards, slaves, and the sons of slaves. The glory of their race was gone. Defeat, disgraceful, overwhelming defeat. They wanted no water nor care for their wounds. They wished only for annihilation, and that their people should not live to hear of their feebleness in war.

Fine men, the odds were nothing to them. Were they not the descendants of the greatest warriors that ever trod the earth? And these soldiers. Alas! alas! Had they not been skulking behind earthworks for nearly a year? Oh, shame! shame! This defeat hardened into steel the whole Maori race. They determined to die hard. But die they now knew they must. Our attack, of course, proceeded in the ordinary way. The big roller crept on nearer and nearer the *pa*. Our men no longer slept in the sap. Large patrols took their place. The Maoris at night tried to destroy our works. The patrols fought them with varying fortunes, and drove them off.

About this time Colonel Warre arrived from India. The general took him out and showed him the Maori position.

"What would you advise, Colonel?"

"Well, you see, I am accustomed to these n——rs. You perceive that little eminence to the right rear? Well, I would seize that, pour in a flanking fire from that position, making a detour to the left with a few companies of men, and then storm the *pa* along that ridge on the right front."

The general gazed at him, and turned nearly green.

"It is an excellent proposal, Colonel. You shall see for yourself."

The general ordered 400 as handsome soldiers as the eye ever rested upon to deploy to the right and seize that little hill. The men advanced gallantly, and then wavered: the Maoris, silent and deadly, were all lying ready in their rifle-pits, each man armed with a double-barrelled smooth-bore. They would have reserved their fire till our men were within forty yards, then delivered a volley at the soldiers' legs, and, skipping out of their rifle-pits, would have disappeared in the forest, leaving a host of our men dead on the field. "What do you say now. Colonel?" The bugles sounded the recall, and we all went back to our fortifications. The soldiers knew the Maoris far better than

Colonel Warre did, and their morale had been damaged by melancholy experience.

Had the general insisted, the men would have carried the position, but at what a loss! Colonel Warre's presence and contemptuous manner were not acceptable to General Pratt. He was sent to take command of the Auckland district.

A MAORI STOREHOUSE

CHAPTER 13

General Cameron

Just at this point, when we were on the eve of rendering Wiremu Kingi's position at Puke-Rangiore untenable, an armistice was sought by Wiremu Tamihana, the King-maker. The Maoris had always got the better of us in diplomacy, and there is little doubt we were outwitted on this occasion. The capture of an empty *pa* meant little to us, and that is all the glory we could have achieved; but the moral effect on the King Movement might have been immense. Nevertheless, our political dissensions were so galling that the armistice was granted. The fact was, most of our South Island Parliamentary representatives, who had suffered nothing, insisted that the war should be prosecuted to the bitter end. In this they were supported by the members from Taranaki, because their homes were devastated and their future gone. The rest of the North Island representatives, supported largely by the Province of Nelson, insisted on peace.

An armistice was the only possible compromise, and it was substantially agreed upon as between independent nations.

General Cameron arrived about this time, and the War Office poured in troops from both India and England. The Maoris foresaw the consequences, and, notwithstanding the arrival of Sir George Grey as Governor—or rather, in consequence of it—both strained every effort to make ready for the final struggle.

General Cameron was in the prime of life. He enjoyed high reputation, was an iron-grey man, a rigid disciplinarian, reticent and austere. His arrival was a surprise dramatically effected. Arriving by steamer, he rode out to Waitara from New Plymouth without giving any notice, handed his authority to General Pratt, and at once took command. I was in medical charge of the field hospital at Waitara. Dressed in a blue jumper, with a pair of brown tweed trousers on tucked into digger's knee-boots, I wore a forage cap with the Army Medical Staff badge. As I was seeing my patients in a large marquee tent, in stalked this military figure. I saluted, and went on dressing the men's wounds.

General Cameron stared at me and said,—

"Are you a medical officer?"

I said, "Yes, General."

He replied, "I could not have thought it."

"Nevertheless, General, it is a fact."

Soon an order was issued for the removal of the headquarters of the 65th Regiment to Auckland. I accompanied it. One day I was walking down Queen Street; it came on to rain, and I found myself sheltering under a verandah with a gentleman in plain clothes, whom I knew to be the general. I respected his *incognito*, and engaged in a general conversation with him. He knew perfectly well who I was. I avoided military subjects, and discussed the social condition of the colony.

He was clearly impressed. Every kind of knowledge was important to him in his difficult position. The shower lifted, and we parted, exchanging the usual courtesies.

The general required just then a report on the housing and sanitary condition of the women and children of some Indian regiments who had just arrived. I was selected for the duty, and sent in a straightforward, businesslike report, urging various concessions outside the prescribed line. This led to my being put in medical charge of a flying column sent to an entirely different part of the colony, where the war had not as yet broken out. Thus, I missed seeing all the important military operations in the Waikato.

When, however, General Cameron moved his headquarters to Wanganui, on the west coast, I received orders to join that expeditionary force. It were bootless to describe the condition of things I found there, or the hardships I underwent. Suffice it to say that the persecutions of the soldier under the cumbersome system in vogue surpassed anything I had previous experience of. General Cameron had loudly declared that New Zealand was the grave of glory—he succeeded in making it an abode of misery for the soldier. Such marching, countermarching, picketing, such a work of double sentries, such an ado to prevent surprises, would have taken the heart out of any man.

The great military strategy was to march all night through slush and rain, in darkness and confusion, and encamp at break of day on some miserable flat reeking with swamp water. How well do I remember an ass of a Colonel commanding a wing of the 68th Foot bawling out constantly, as we floundered through the tangled roots and mud in the darkness of the winter's night, "Keep your fours, men!" and the reply in a strident voice, "Ah, then, is it all fours you mean, Colonel?"

I have said enough. I went through months of it, and had it not been for a sense of humour strong in me, I sometimes think I would have died under the hardship.

CHAPTER 14

From Cameron to Chute

Notwithstanding all our precautions, a handful of gallant Maoris worked through our pickets at Nukumaru, and surprised a body of men in the very heart of our encampment. Lieutenant Gudgeon, in his *New Zealand War*, says a Maori was shot just outside the general's tent. If so, that incident was kept secret. I was encamped there at the time with the 68th Foot, and beyond the fact that there had been a surprise, I heard nothing. After this incident our precautions seemed to be redoubled. Dull care sat enthroned over the whole force. The soldiers, though physically powerful and in excellent health, were spiritless. There was nothing but drudgery; no fighting to stir the pulses of the men. We marched past the Wereroa *pa*, leaving it on our right. It was said to be impregnable. Finally, we encamped at the mouth of the Patea River. Here we made asses of ourselves—marching about through high fern up to our shoulders, and never moving except in overwhelming numbers.

One fine day, with the sun shining gladly overhead, we set out, a great force of us, horse, foot, and artillery. Forming a halfmoon, with the cavalry skirmishing on the right and left flanks, we advanced over an open plain to Kakaramea.

The village of Kakaramea was situated on a gentle hill sloping to the plain. A flax and *toi-toi* swamp lay at the foot of Kakaramea, and extended in depth about a mile to our front as we advanced. The Maoris, about 120 men, women, and boys, came out to meet us under the protection of this cover. We swooped down upon them. Their prospect was hopeless; we had them completely in our power. This made no difference to the Maori. He fought in the open, delivering his fire, retired slowly loading in a dignified manner. The women fought beside the men, the boys in front of all. The dignity and martial

215

bearing of the Maoris touched the hearts of our soldiers. Very few of the Maoris were killed, and the wounded were handled with infinite tenderness by our men. The majority of the defenders of Kakaramea got away scatheless, and everyone on our side was equally delighted. The British soldier's heart was not in the struggle.

I heard our men say, "Begorra, it's a murder to shoot them. Sure, they are our own people, with their potatoes, and fish, and children. Who knows but that they are Irishmen, with faces a little darkened by the sun, who escaped during the persecutions of Cromwell?"

The wounded Maoris and white men were all collected together in the *nunanga*-house at the top of the hill in the village. They were treated in turn by the surgeons of the force, according to the gravity of their injuries, irrespective of rank or colour. When the wounded were all seen to. General Cameron, a man of the most humane disposition, visited the *nunanga*-house, making affectionate inquiries and giving expression to soothing words. I happened to be present. When the general's interpreter came opposite one Maori, I said, "General, that is a most extraordinary man. He has received two gunshot wounds; his thigh has already been amputated, and his arm is in danger; he has had the bayonet thrust into his body seven times, and received four sabre wounds in the head. Look at him now, smoking his pipe as tranquilly as a baby sucking a bottle."

The interpreter interpreted all I had said to the Maori. He nodded his head, and smiled in a sweet and gentle manner.

The general's eyes moistened, and he became a little pale.

"In the name of God," he exclaimed, "why did you resist our advance? Could you not see we were in overwhelming force?"

The Maori replied, "What would you have us do? This is our village, these are our plantations. Men are not fit to live if not brave enough to defend their own homes."

The general looked abashed. "At any rate," he said, "I am glad to see you are now well treated. Have you any complaints to make?"

"No. . . . By the way, yes. Whilst I was lying wounded on the ground, and after a soldier had given me a drink, an officer came up and sabred me."

"That is not according to the usages of war."

"That is a slave's work."

The general turned purple and swore an oath. "I'll cashier him. Would you know the man?"

"Yes. I was a little flurried, but I would know the man."

There was a great turmoil in the camp; hot and fevered inquiries. Presently a colour-sergeant marched in, holding a drummer-boy by the ear. The boy was marched up opposite the Maori, who continued to smoke and gaze at him intently,

"Is that the officer?"

"Yes," said the Maori; "that is he."

The interpreter explained that the youth was a drummer-boy, and his sword was only a toy.

"Do not say any more about it," quoth the Maori. "Boys must be boys. We train our own sons the same way."

It seems to be the only fashion we have in common.

This Maori recovered, and was set free. He went to war against us afresh on his return to his people. He was taken prisoner in a surprise effected by Colonel McDonnell, and when I saw him, he smiled on me, and we exchanged confidences.

"What!" I said, "in arms again?"

"Yes," he said. "What would you have a man do? He must stand by his own people."

Our whole force after this became listless. An idea prevailed that it was an unjust war, in every way discreditable to us. The soldier no longer desired to kill the Maoris, and disliked more than ever being killed by him. In spite of a most harassing discipline, it became in some instances a task to muster the men for picket duty. It is a fact that I often heard commented on, that in one regiment it took the non-commissioned officers twenty to thirty minutes to muster a complement of fifty men for outpost duty. The heart had gone out of the enterprise, when unexpectedly General Cameron gave up the command, and General Chute succeeded him.

General Chute was considered one of the best drills in Her Majesty's service. The soldiers christened him the "Kerry Bull," not merely from his resonant voice, which on parade echoed from hill to hill, but on account of his general appearance and roaming disposition. He was a short-legged man, with a shaggy, square, masculine head and powerful body. He walked deliberately, carrying his head a little to either side, and no man could precisely foretell his temper from day to day. He was equally loved and feared by his own regiment, but as he was not a scientific soldier, and naturally of a retiring disposition, he was little known to the army generally.

Owing to the weight of his body and short grip of his legs, he was a poor equestrian. Consequently, he rode a quiet old horse, whose hair was left as long as possible, because the general was equally short-tempered and good-natured. When anything went wrong on parade, the general swore awfully, and hammered his old horse with a short hunting-crop,—treatment which made the animal play curious tricks. The whole spectacle was something to marvel at, but no one who looked at the general's face could have the hardihood to laugh and expect to survive.

When he took command, I saw at once he was a character, and soon became convinced he was as lonely as a moulting crow in the midst of his predecessor's brilliant staff. I therefore watched him closely. I was sufficiently known and sufficiently insignificant to be able to do this without attracting attention. The general, however, by a curious intuitive power some men possess, saw under my grave, respectful demeanour a certain humorous sympathy with his difficult position. He always had the habit of walking about amongst the men. Alone, and wearing a shabby undress uniform, whacking his riding-boot with his hunting-crop, he would turn up anywhere in the camp.

The men liked their rough, capable commander. In a few days they sang and whistled and joked each other with all the zest of a newly recovered gaiety, marching light-heartedly with a swing in their gait.

I had previously resigned my commission, with a view to settling in the colony. On providing a substitute I was allowed to retire on leave, so I saw no more of General Chute's expedition. A field officer, however, of Crimean experience, continued the observations I had always made, and this is the narrative he told me about five months afterwards:—

Soon after your departure we had a brush with the enemy. The soldiers went into it with heart, so we were successful everywhere. The general walked about the camp, chatting with the men. 'Jolly fine sport we have had this morning, boys; plenty of pigs and potatoes and poultry after it' We had captured an open village, and were rejoicing over the enemy's supplies. 'A good feed tonight—a short, tight sleep—an early march in the morning—another fight about the break of day. Donnybrook will be nothing to it,'

The men merely smiled, and rejoiced openly when his back was turned. It was decided to march round Mount Egmont Dr. Featherston, Superintendent of the Province of Wellington, arrived with 300 friendly natives. The general profoundly distrusted friendly natives.

Isaac Earle Featherston was a stern, strong, haughty man, with a genial nature when not irritated. Proud and self-reliant, he resented dictation of any kind. General Chute and he jarred whenever they met. The general ordered the natives to parade before the break of day, make a detour through the forest, and take a *pa* he was about to attack in the rear.

Dr. Featherston said the Maoris were weary and footsore from constant marching; that to be hurried in this way was contrary to their tribal custom; that they were most useful allies, but must be humoured a bit.

General Chute lost his temper; said, 'Damn you and your allies! If they do not march when I order them, I will fire into them. I will have no mutiny in my camp, supported by the civil authority.'

Chute marched off, and left Featherston in a rage. Featherston sat down and smoked cheroot after cheroot, saying nothing. This was a bad sign. Featherston silent was a dangerous man.

Now, there was an officer in camp, Deputy-Commissary-General Strickland. The success of this expedition was everything to him. It meant promotion and a C.B. Strickland was a man of great Eastern experience. He saw what was going on, and said, 'This will never do.' He called on Featherston, who sat smoking in his tent, asked for something to drink, and lit his pipe. Featherston knew him, and liked Strickland's rugged humour.

"Strickland at length said, 'The general has sent me to ask you to supper.'

Featherston exploded.

'It is like General Chute's damned insolence! As soon as the war is over, I will call him out and shoot him, I wish to the Almighty every soldier in the colony was out of it. Were it not for my duty to New Zealand, I would fall upon General Chute's force this night with my Maoris and slaughter the whole of his men.'

Strickland smoked on, and made no reply until Featherston's volcanic eruption was over. Then he said—

'The general recognises the full force or what you have said. He will give you ample satisfaction when the time comes. All the same, there is no use in two men like you quarrelling now. The general knows that he cannot get on without you. His temper is the curse of his life, but he is a very good fellow, and you will like him well when you know him as I do. May I tell him you will come to supper?'

Featherston mused a bit, and said—

'I will think of it.'

Strickland then went to General Chute and said—

'I have just been with Featherston. He desires me to say he is coming to supper with you.'

'The devil he is!'

'Yes, General; and, look here, you may as well ask me too.'

Chute did ask Strickland. Strickland at the proper moment went over, and said—

'Featherston, the general is waiting supper for you.'

They all three supped together, rose from table immense friends, and the friendship was permanent.

I will now narrate precisely, and almost word for word, the exact story I heard of the attack on Otapawa from a field-officer of distinction who served there. This account was verified in every detail by a private of the 14th Foot, who was present and took part in the attack.

When the 57th Foot were ordered to assault Otapawa, which was a fortified, rifle-pitted *pa*, they rushed forward with great gallantry, supported by the 14th Foot. The slope which led to the *pa* had been scarped, and when the men were within 150 yards of the stockade, they met such a deadly volley that they wavered.

General Chute rode up, whacking his old horse with his riding-crop; swore and blasphemed in an awful manner. At last he became silent for a moment; then he stood up in his stirrups, and said—

You do not know me, men. I am Billy Chute. Do you think you are going to make a laughing-stock of me at every club in Pall Mall? I swear by the living God I will leave the bones of the whole army to bleach on the sides of these mountains before I will ever turn my back on any fortification I once assault. Fifty-Seventh, I will do worse than that: I will disgrace you before the whole army. Fourteenth, charge!

The 14th had a vile reputation for discipline; but this regiment knew the "Kerry Bull." They uttered one fearful yell, and sought to break past the 57th. The 57th rushed headlong at the *pa*, and these two regiments almost bayoneted each other in their eagerness to get in first. The Maoris broke in terror at the fury of the assault, and never again faced the bayonet.

The 14th Foot and the 57th were not encamped near each other for some time after this, and the officers and men of both regiments, knowing the gravity of the position, kept perfectly silent, never even discussing amongst themselves this incident.

Chapter 15

Ropata and the Hau-Haus

On retiring from Her Majesty's service, I was appointed to make an inspection of the Army Medical Department of the Colonial forces. This brought me into close contact with a new set of men. I shall not enlarge upon my own adventures and hairbreadth 'scapes. It is sufficient to say that, though insignificant, they were quite startling enough for a man of my prudent turn of mind. My object is to sketch a contrast. For this purpose, I need only confine myself to bare narrative.

I arrived at Waiapu, on the east coast of the North Island, where Major Fraser was in command of about a hundred Europeans and as many friendly Maoris as for the time cared to join in the consumption of his supplies.

We marched in the dark, so as to arrive soon after the break of day at the enemy's fortified *pa*, Puke-Marire. We found it perched on a hill, skirted by forest on each side, open and easy of access in the front. Major Fraser took up a position about 400 yards to the front of the *pa*, and threw his handful of men out in skirmishing order, giving instructions that no man must venture beyond prescribed limits, which were carefully pointed out The Colonial troops opened fire. The friendly Maoris sat down at a secure distance to watch events. Major Fraser folded his arms and walked up and down like the captain of a ship, occasionally examining the position with his glasses.

One of our men had advanced too near the *pa* on our right front. The major sent a corporal and two men to fetch him back. He was marched back between sentries, and when brought face to face with the commanding officer, he commenced cursing and swearing in the most voluble manner. Major Fraser dismissed the corporal and his guard, and took no notice whatever of the prisoner. This made the worthy colonist more furious than ever. He tore off his cartouche-box, hurled it on the ground, rammed his bayonet up to the muzzle of the rifle into the earth, danced upon his forage-cap, called Major Fraser a white-livered sneak, who, afraid to fight himself, would not let anyone else do it for him.

Major Fraser walked impassively up and down like a deaf-mute. The colonist could make nothing of this, so he presently took out his pipe, lit it, sat down, and had a smoke.

I watched this man when the fun really began. He snatched up his rifle, seized his cartouche-box, and, forgetting both his forage-cap and his anger, rushed with all speed lest any other fellow should get into the *pa* before him.

Well, all I can say is, the whole affair was quite unlike anything I had ever seen before. When the word was given, every man fought for himself; and though they were all well forward, there was little for the enemy to fire at. My attention was diverted from the advance of the Europeans by the arrival of our allies, the Ngatiporou, under Major Ropata. They advanced at full speed in a solid square, with their bayonets aloft glittering in the sun. They ran for hundreds of yards, without breaking their formation, and then in a moment scattered like a flock of birds. I was my own master, so I pelted after them as fast as I could run. They took to the forest on our left. After a toilsome chase, I overtook them. They were now established at the rear of the enemy's position.

Here the Puke-Marire *pa* fell sheer to the river, and towered above us about thirty or forty feet. The rock was of a soft sandstone formation. As we stood at the foot of this precipice, we were safe from the *Hau-Haus*: their fire passed over us. Major Ropata instructed some of his men to climb the forest trees, where, under the shelter of the spreading branches, they acted as sharpshooters. The rest of the force set to work with axes, and cut zig-zag steps in the sandstone.

As soon as this was done, men mounted, and about five feet six from the level of the *pa*, which was built close to the precipice, they cut out a junk lengthways, about eight or ten inches deep. They worked upwards at this until they could look over and fire straight into the enemy's rifle-pits. A body of men now occupied this vantage-ground. At the word of command, they all loaded. Then the right-hand man sang out, "Hi! Ha! Hau!" At the final word, "Hau!" each Ngatiporou placed his rifle above his head, resting it on the bank in front of him, and pulled the trigger. The result was a uniform close volley.

This tactic was renewed again and again, till invariably at the word

"*Hau!*" the hostile Maori ducked his head, and disappeared in his rifle-pit. At a given moment when the word "*Hau!*" was heard, the Ngatiporou diverged their fire to the right and left, leaving a V-shaped space secure in the middle. A small Maori boy, furnished with a hawser, jumped on to that area of safety, and, making weird movements of defiance, cast the loop of the hawser over a large post of the stockade, and then jumped over the precipice, and was caught by his waiting tribe.

A noble-looking antagonist, with shaggy head and glittering eye, rose with an axe to cut away the loop of this hawser. He was shot dead by one of Ropata's men perched in an adjacent tree. The bulk of Ropata's men at the base of the precipice hauled on the hawser, while the sharpshooters from the trees and the men on the ledge poured in a deadly fire on the enemy. Ropata now found a drain at the right angle of our position of assault. It had been cut to let the storm-water run freely off the *pa* into the river.

Into this drain Ropata crept, till he got inside the fortification. Here he seized his nearest unsuspecting enemy by the feet, dragged him out, and hurled him down to his tribe, who danced a war-dance; then at the word of command scaled the precipice like swarming bees, rushed through the breach where the beam had given way, and carried the whole position on that side as the Europeans entered on the other. Nearly all the enemy got into the forest, as they knew well the crucial moment for flight. Except for the moral effect, the victory was of little value, for the hostile Maoris merely ran away to fight again.

In point of fact, the Maori war wore itself out as the charm of the national and religious sentiment became attenuated. No armies could conquer such a people in such a country. Food was all the time practically abundant, and unless you exterminated the whole race, you could not wipe out their feverish ambition and restless, imaginative self-confidence. The Maoris never had any quarrel with the colonists, who in their hearts loved and respected the fierce spirit of independence which is the chief characteristic of this wonderful race.

It must ever remain a monument to the wisdom and humanity of the Parliament of New Zealand that it succeeded in securing and maintaining the confidence of such a people.

It must not be forgotten that there were two epochs in the war—the National movement under Wiremu Tamihana, the King-maker, and the wave of religious enthusiasm called "*Hau-hauism*" which followed it. The Imperial troops broke the back of the National movement both in Taranaki and Waikato. The Colonial troops with their

Native allies saw the religious fever flicker and die. The Maori race remains, and competes in the field of intellect and athletics to this day.

If the truth were known, the New Zealanders were more proud of their Maori contingent in the late Jubilee procession in London than of anything else, except their own Anglo-Saxon blood. The New Zealanders hold they are the first people who, neither conquerors of nor conquered by a coloured race, have made them friends and equals to the advantage of all.

On leaving Waiapu, I went to Opotiki, where Mr. Volckner had been murdered. Here I fell in for the first time with Colonel McDonnell in his new character of soldier and Maori captain. I saw his contingent go into action, and was much struck by the novelty of the method.

Colonel McDonnell, armed with a breech-loader, started out in a rough country at the rate of about five miles an hour, personally to engage the enemy. His Maori soldiers kept up to him as well as they could in a long "gypsy streel." As soon as the engagement commenced, nothing could restrain Colonel McDonnell's zeal. He was at the head of everything; led in a series of personal encounters of which the battle consisted, and seemed to carry a charmed life. The native chiefs on McDonnell's side vied with him in personal gallantry, and the common men filled up the space anyhow.

The singular good temper with which the antagonists killed each other in this encounter was the chief feature. If the wrong man happened to be shot by the wrong side, there was not much fuss about it. It seemed to be all in the day's work.

When the battle was over, there was discussion about tomahawking the wounded; but McDonnell put an end to all that by tapping the butt of his breech-loader and looking mighty dangerous. Our Maoris soon discovered that the wounded "Hau-haus" were really their close relations, and took as much care of them as if they were new playthings just discovered by children. The wounded, with the singular placidity of the race, took battle, wounds, petting and all as if they had been accustomed to it, and gave without stint valuable information as to the numbers and disposition of the enemy. By chatting with these men, I got their account of the Volckner incident.

The singular thing about a Maoris is that he always talks without bias, in a perfectly calm, philosophic spirit. This arises from the fact that his intellect is cultivated from childhood. The life is in common, and the smallest bairn has the right to enter into discussions touching

225

KEREOPA, WHO SWALLOWED VOLCKER'S EYES

the affairs of his *hapu*, or tribe.

"Why did you murder Volckner?"

"We executed him according to law. He was fairly tried in our *runanga*-house, openly confronted with his own letters giving information to the soldiers, our enemies. He was one of our people; we had adopted him into our tribe. He acknowledged the adoption, and lived with us for many years. He was a traitor, and we hanged him according to the law of nations."

"But Kereopa tore out the dead man's eyes, and swallowed them!"

"There is nothing in that. There is no difference between a dead man's and a dead fish's eye. As Kereopa swallowed the right eye, he said, 'This is the Queen.' Of the left eye he said, 'This is the Parliament.' It was only a symbol."

CHAPTER 16

Beguiling the Ngatipukeka

It became necessary for me to reach Tauranga, in order to return to Wellington. I informed Colonel McDonnell of this fact, and asked him for a horse and a guide. He explained to me the journey had its dangers, because the hostile Maoris occupied the country between Opotiki and Maketu. He promised to send out spies and let me know when the track might be reasonably considered safe. I noticed that his spies were all women.

At one time he would say, "If you start at once, the road will be found comparatively safe." In a quarter of an hour he would send word, "Emma has just come in, and reports an ambush at the river mouth." Then in ten minutes, "Martha informs me that the *Hau-Haus* have retired to the forest."

My reply was always the same: "My dear McDonnell, give the word, and I am off. I will take whatever risk you consider reasonable."

At length a Maori boy appeared, leading a starved-looking wild horse. The horse had on a halter-bridle and an old saddle with a stirrup on one side and a piece of rope, as a substitute, on the other. The boy was mounted bareback, with a loop of rope round his horse's nose.

McDonnell said, "Now, start at once, and gallop along the sea beach! Once you have crossed the river, which is only five or six miles distant, you may strike inland, and will be comparatively safe."

Maori horses always travel with their heads up in the air, and gallop recklessly as long as they have a leg under them. Away we went, the Maori boy leading. We very soon arrived at the river, which at the mouth looked about 150 yards wide, and was in flood. The boy dismounted and hunted up and down the river for a canoe. After a time, he returned and said, "The canoe has been washed away. The river is too high and broad for these horses to carry us over. We must either return or travel inland in search of a ford."

We travelled up the bank of the river for miles. At length we saw a practical ford. We were half-way across when Maoris in numbers came running towards us.

I cried out in a loud voice, according to Maoris custom—

"How are you? How are you all? It is a great pleasure to see you!"

This rather staggered the Ngatipukeka. I had just dropped into their power. They had not spoken to a white man since the death of Volckner. I rode straight up, and shook hands with many of them, then dismounted and handed the halter of my horse to a youth who stood near. The Maoris looked much surprised, and immediately assembled in numbers to gratify their curiosity, and hear the news. I wore a sword over my waterproof coat, and had on a forage cap with V.R. on it in large gold letters. As they evidently expected me to say something, I looked wise and solemn, and told them to collect all their people for a talk in the afternoon. This quite satisfied them. I then moved about amongst the people and made friends. In particular, I sought to ingratiate myself with the women, so as to extract from their talk some inkling of the public feeling.

Whilst walking about and chatting, I studied with minute attention the facial expression of each male adult Maori I came in contact with. At length I picked out a man I considered trustworthy, and secretly handed him a flask of spirits I carried in my breast pocket. This was a propitiatory offering, and he took it as such.

About four o'clock in the afternoon a large wood fire was lit. An old marquee tent, evidently carried off from our men as the result of some sudden surprise, was pitched to the leeward of the fire. My place was allotted in front of the tent door. The most important chiefs were seated to my right and left, and the tribe generally—men, women and children—completed the circle. Dead silence prevailed. It was clear I was expected to speak. I knew better than that. I had often seen Donald McLean at these *runangas*, and I knew that a great chief must cultivate silence and imperturbability. It is the custom at these meetings for the least important people to speak first. My object was to gain time, study the attitude and temper of the Ngatipukeka, and frame my address to suit it.

Speeches were delivered for about an hour and a half. The chief men both on my right and left had spoken, and the temper of the tribe had been played upon, according to the varying humour of the orators.

I rose, and said—

"Salutations to you, O Ngatipukeka! I have come from Wellington. Governor Grey is sad at the slaughter of his children of both races. There has been enough fighting. Let us have peace, and live in brotherly contentment. It has not been the custom of great tribes to fight for ever. You have had satisfaction; we have had satisfaction. Let the dead on each side rise up, and attest this truth. I have spoken."

Complete silence followed. Then up rose a chief, whose bitter hostility I had noted from the beginning.

"What the Queen's officer says may be well. But what about the Arawa? They are now all armed with rifles, well-fed and equipped. The Europeans are their friends. The sea is open to them for supplies. Once peace is made, the soldiers will be withdrawn to England. The Arawas will fall upon us, and our fate will be hard indeed. Already they have driven off all our cattle. The soldiers guard the Maketu River; we cannot recover them. What does the *Pakeha* say?"

I arose, and, gazing around with sneering lip and distended nostril, said—

"Ah, great is the wisdom of the council-chief; far-reaching his guile; deep as the ocean his love for his people. Has he forgotten that the Arawas, even with the assistance of the soldiers, could not conquer the Ngatipukeka? Is he not aware that, in order to steal cattle, the Arawa had to come like thieves in the night—not like warriors in the morning? Once peace with the Europeans is made, ask your war-chiefs whether the Arawa will not fade away before your valour, as their ancestors did. I have spoken. Yet great is the *Pakeha's* admiration for the courage of your tribe. Write now a letter challenging the Arawa to meet you in combat. I will deliver it in person. Send a detachment of your men with me. Once landed on the opposite bank of the river, I shall hurl defiance at the Arawa in your name. *Kati*— enough."

I had outflanked the wily old devil, and he knew it. Food was served; wild pig, potatoes, and tea, made of the leaf of the ti-tree. At length numbers of us crowded into the tent, and slept like herrings in a tin case.

About two o'clock there was an alarm. First, I felt my revolver, thinking my last hour had come. Soon I perceived the tent was on fire. The fire was extinguished, but the tent was destroyed. We all lay down on the ground. Soon it began to rain, and soaked us to the bone. We arose in the morning, and I was summoned by a council of chiefs to consider the terms of the challenge to the Arawa. My enemy was there. I knew by instinct he had drafted the challenge. The pen used was a sharpened stick. The ink had been made of moistened powder.

I read the challenge with an air of much scorn, laid it down, took it up again, carefully studied every word of it, altering the expression of my countenance from scorn to deep, unimpassioned thought. I knew I had my antagonist in an agony of solicitude. I had destroyed his wisdom last night. What might I not do this morning? After much anxious thought I said, "It is good." I had secured the friendship of the writer. My life was safe.

I folded up the challenge, which was written on a piece of cartridge-paper, in my pocket case. The council broke up, and I retired alone. On my way I met the Maori to whom I had given my spirit-flask the day before. He made a sign to me, and I accompanied him into the scrub. Once there, he took from under his mat my spirit-flask, and handed it back to me. I said—

"Keep it: it is for you."

He said, "Unscrew the top."

I did so. The liquor had not been touched I was amazed. Here was a man who had not tasted liquor for years, and yet, out of delicacy for my position, had resisted the temptation during such a night. I said—

"Drink!"

He replied: "No. You are a stranger and a guest. No man would do such a thing."

I said: "It is yours, not mine. Drink."

He said: "Drink first, then."

I did so, merely tasting it, then handed him the flask. He emptied it at a draught.

"Keep the flask in memory of me."

He did so, and we parted.

Accompanied by an escort, I rode to the Maketu River. There dismounting, I approached the bank, and taking out a white handkerchief waved it for some time. My escort stood back under cover of some scrub. Soon the Arawa sent over a canoe. On arrival at the opposite shore, I handed the Arawa the Ngatipukeka challenge My escort came forth and danced defiance on their bank. The Arawa responded in kind. The incident was over: I was safe.

COUNCIL CHIEF OF THE NGATIPUKEKA

CHAPTER 17

Sir George Grey and General Chute

The great difficulty experienced by General Cameron in conducting the war consisted in the intricate series of obstacles put in his way by Governor Grey. Sir George Grey was an extremely polished, gentlemanly, handsome man, with a soft manner and a seething volcano for a heart. He hated General Cameron, with the cold, concentrated rage of a self-devouring nature. I could tell you precisely the why and wherefore, were I in a confidential mood. I am only concerned now with my final interview with General Chute. I met him in Wellington. He came forward, and said—

"Well, how is your good lady?"

(He was himself still a bachelor.)

"Very well, indeed, thank you. General, By the way, General, how did you get on with Sir George Grey?"

"I had no trouble with him whatever."

"How did you manage?"

"Sir George always sent for me, and said, 'You know, General, we must do so and so, and so and so.'

"I replied, 'Yes, Your Excellency.'

"He invariably wound up by saying, 'Now, General, you thoroughly understand the policy unfolded and the plan of campaign?' And I replied, 'Yes, Your Excellency.'

"As soon as I had gone away, I sat down and wrote him the following letter:—

To His Excellency,
Sir George Grey, K.C.B.,
Commander-in-Chief of Her Majesty's
Naval and Military Forces.

Sir,—

I have the honour to inform you I am troubled with a very bad memory, and I have quite forgotten all you said to me, and will you be good enough to put your instructions in writing?

I have, etc.,

Trevor Chute,
Major-General.

"He never put anything in writing, and I did whatever I liked; and so, you see, I finished the campaign in a few months."

CHAPTER 18

Conclusion

The New Zealand War lasted about ten years. It might well have lasted another seven, had it not been for the good sense of the Maoris.

What can a civilized nation do with a race which considers the most extraordinary achievements easy and natural? We had about one hundred and twenty Maoris imprisoned in a hulk, anchored miles out of Wellington Harbour. These were men Colonel McDonnell had taken as prisoners. Amongst them was the one-legged hero of Ka-karamea, whose story I told on a former occasion. One very stormy night a strong nor'-wester was blowing. The sea was washed into foam, and the waves were breaking over the old hulk as she lay at anchor. The military guard being for the most part comfortably asleep, the Maoris slid one by one out of the porthole, and drifted with the wind to Nghauranga, swimming a distance of about four miles.

Their chief was old and feeble, so their strongest men took it in turns to support him in the water. Some of their bravest were worn out and drowned in this heroic service. The whole of the prisoners, including the old chief and the one-legged hero of Kakaramea, with the exception of five who were drowned in the struggle to save their chief, landed in safety, and had so effectually disappeared by daylight that we never saw any more of them.

The Maoris were never conquered. They might have been ex-terminated—conquered in a military sense, no. They realised that a Maori kingdom in which the White Man should be subject to the Maoris had become an impossibility, and therefore ceased fighting.

As a race they had never despised or hated the White Man. They determined as a piece of statecraft to become one with the white people, and they have succeeded in every particular. The Maori never faltered with his self-respect No single Maori ever betrayed his race.

The Maori made the best of his position, took all he could get, and yielded as little as possible. For all practical purposes we are one people and proud to remain so; and certainly, neither in intellect, physique, nor morals can the Maoris well be considered our inferiors. Unfortunately, they are not our equals in sustained industry. If they fail to correct that deficiency, they must go under. We shall be the first to mourn their fall.

LEONAUR

ALSO FROM LEONAUR
AVAILABLE IN SOFTCOVER OR HARDCOVER WITH DUST JACKET

ZULU:1879 *by D.C.F. Moodie & the Leonaur Editors*—The Anglo-Zulu War of 1879 from contemporary sources: First Hand Accounts, Interviews, Dispatches, Official Documents & Newspaper Reports.

THE RED DRAGOON *by W.J. Adams*—With the 7th Dragoon Guards in the Cape of Good Hope against the Boers & the Kaffir tribes during the 'war of the axe' 1843-48'.

THE RECOLLECTIONS OF SKINNER OF SKINNER'S HORSE *by James Skinner*—James Skinner and his 'Yellow Boys' Irregular cavalry in the wars of India between the British, Mahratta, Rajput, Mogul, Sikh & Pindarree Forces.

A CAVALRY OFFICER DURING THE SEPOY REVOLT *by A. R. D. Mackenzie*—Experiences with the 3rd Bengal Light Cavalry, the Guides and Sikh Irregular Cavalry from the outbreak to Delhi and Lucknow.

A NORFOLK SOLDIER IN THE FIRST SIKH WAR *by J W Baldwin*—Experiences of a private of H.M. 9th Regiment of Foot in the battles for the Punjab, India 1845-6.

TOMMY ATKINS' WAR STORIES: 14 FIRST HAND ACCOUNTS—Fourteen first hand accounts from the ranks of the British Army during Queen Victoria's Empire.

THE WATERLOO LETTERS *by H. T. Siborne*—Accounts of the Battle by British Officers for its Foremost Historian.

NEY: GENERAL OF CAVALRY VOLUME 1—1769-1799 *by Antoine Bulos*—The Early Career of a Marshal of the First Empire.

NEY: MARSHAL OF FRANCE VOLUME 2—1799-1805 *by Antoine Bulos*—The Early Career of a Marshal of the First Empire.

AIDE-DE-CAMP TO NAPOLEON *by Philippe-Paul de Ségur*—For anyone interested in the Napoleonic Wars this book, written by one who was intimate with the strategies and machinations of the Emperor, will be essential reading.

TWILIGHT OF EMPIRE *by Sir Thomas Ussher & Sir George Cockbum*—Two accounts of Napoleon's Journeys in Exile to Elba and St. Helena: Narrative of Events by Sir Thomas Ussher & Napoleon's Last Voyage: Extract of a diary by Sir George Cockburn.

PRIVATE WHEELER *by William Wheeler*—The letters of a soldier of the 51st Light Infantry during the Peninsular War & at Waterloo.

Lightning Source UK Ltd.
Milton Keynes UK
UKHW010655111220
374994UK00007B/105

9 781782 828730